Organizational Project Management

Linking Strategy and Projects

Edited by

Rosemary Hossenlopp, PMP

MANAGEMENTCONCEPTS

ſſſ
MANAGEMENTCONCEPTS

8230 Leesburg Pike, Suite 800
Vienna, VA 22182
(703) 790-9595
Fax: (703) 790-1371
www.managementconcepts.com

Printed in the United States of America

Library of Congress Cataloging-in-Publication Data

Organizational project management : linking strategy and projects / edited by
Rosemary Hossenlopp.
     p. cm.
  ISBN 978-1-56726-282-7
1. Project management. 2. Strategic planning. I. Hossenlopp, Rosemary, 1958-
HD69.P75O74 2010
658.4'04--dc22

                                                                    2010013853

10   9   8   7   6   5   4   3   2   1

■ ABOUT THE EDITOR

Rosemary Hossenlopp, MBA, PMP, has focused on new-product introductions and IT project management in top Silicon Valley firms for 20 years. Her key focus areas are project management offices, assessments, and project requirements. She is a speaker, consultant, and trainer for commercial, federal, and state organizations.

Rosemary received her BS from Oregon State University and her MBA from Santa Clara University. She is an adjunct professor at UCSC Extension in Silicon Valley, a Project Management Professional (PMP), a featured blogger on the UCSC Extension Project Management website and on the Information Systems Special Interest Group (PMI-ISSIG®) website (http://www.pmi-issig.org), and a founding volunteer member of the Project Management Institute's Organizational Project Management Virtual Community (http://opm.community.pmi.org). She is the coauthor of *Unearthing Business Requirements* and a contributor to the Institute of Business Analysis Body of Knowledge. Her website is www.PM-Prespectives.com.

▌ ABOUT THE AUTHORS

Abdur Rafay Badar, PMP, OPM3® Consultant, founder of Emilia CNFM LLC, Dubai (www.emiliallc.com) is a computer engineer with 17 years of international experience in business development, project management, sales, software development, and the installation and commissioning of information technology and instrumentation and controls solutions in industrial and nonindustrial environments. He has been living in Dubai for the past nine years and has been involved in teaching and conducting courses at American University of Sharjah, Sir Syed University of Engineering, University of Idaho, and the PMI-AGC chapter. He holds an MBA from Preston University.

Marcia Daszko is a catalyst for strategic change, transformation, and innovation. For almost 20 years, she has worked with executive teams in commercial settings, government agencies, and nonprofit organizations. Guiding transformative, adaptive change is Marcia's passion.

Marcia is a keynote speaker at conferences and facilitates and teaches at executive retreats. A protégé of Dr. W. Edwards Deming, she founded two Deming users groups and assisted in 20 of the late Dr. Deming's renowned four-day seminars. She is a founding board member of the non-profit In2:InThinking Network, which holds an annual forum, now in its eighth year. She has taught graduate classes at UC Berkeley, Fordham University, and San Jose State University. She is the author of the book *Survival Is Optional*, which is scheduled for publication in 2010, and her website is www.mdaszko.com.

Folake Dosunmu, PMP, PgMP, OPM3® Consultant, is founder of Enovate Masters, Inc., and is an educator and conference speaker. She has more than 20 years of global management experience, specializing in organizational transformation initiatives, project assessments, and project management. She speaks at conferences on topics related to business transformation, change management, portfolio and project management, and the *Organizational Project Management Maturity Model* (OPM3®). She holds a master's degree in organizational leadership.

Randall Englund, NPDP, CBM, is an author, speaker, trainer, professional facilitator, and executive consultant for the Englund Project Management Consultancy (www.englundpmc.com). He draws upon experiences as a former senior project manager with Hewlett-Packard Company for 22 years. He is the author of three best-selling books in the business and management field and is a frequent seminar presenter for the Project Management Institute.

Pavan Kumar Gorakavi, CAPM, works as a senior software developer in Dallas. He supports the project management profession as a VP of programs for asapm Young Crew, which prepares project managers for success, and is an associate director of marketing for PMI-ISSIG®. He is an author of a book published in India on artificial intelligence and digital electronics. His research interests are artificial intelligence, agile methodologies, and software development. He holds a master's degree in computer science and an MBA.

Russ McDowell, M. Eng., PMP, OPM3® Assessor/Consultant, is an independent consultant specializing in program/project management and business development. He has been involved in the setup or management of many project offices, the definition of project management frameworks, and the management of many successful projects. He works in both government and nongovernment organizations and is an active speaker in PMI symposiums and local Institute of Electronics and Electronics Engineers (IEEE) management chapters. His website is www.russona.com.

He has been cited in three of the PMI® global standards for his active role in the initial development of key standards in the area of organizational project management. Russ has a master's degree in systems engineering.

Sara Núñez, PMP, OPM3® Assessor/Consultant, is a leader in organizational development effectiveness, using project, program, and portfolio management integrated solutions to improve business strategy performance at all levels of an organization. She has experience in operations management, information systems, marketing, product development, and business reengineering in the telecommunications and high-tech industries. She has worked with well-known companies such as Verizon, Intel, UBS Financial Services, and AT&T Wireless Services.

Sara performed OPM assessment in Latino-America countries such as Chile, Colombia, and Mexico including work with universities to establish project management educational curriculums. She holds a master's degree in project management from George Washington University.

Michael O'Brochta, MPM, PMP, owner and president of Zozer Inc., has been a project manager for over 30 years and is also an experienced line manager, author, lecturer, trainer, and consultant. As a senior project manager in the U.S. Central Intelligence Agency, he led the maturation of project management practices agency-wide. He helps organizations raise their level of project management performance, which includes leading the development of courses for the Federal Acquisition Institute in support of the new governmentwide Federal Acquisition Certification for Program and Project Managers (FAC-P/PM).

Since his recent climb of another of the world's seven summits, he has been exploring the relationship between project management and mountain climbing. He presents frequently at PMI national, international, and regional conferences. He holds a master's degree in project management.

Raju Rao is a senior project management professional based in India. He is particularly interested in understanding the relationship between strategy and projects, Organizational Project Management, and applying these concepts for a nation's progress. He often speaks at Global congresses and is a correspondent for PM Forum for India. Raju has been involved in the development of many standards of PMI, including OPM3®.

He is a PMP, Stanford Certified Project Manager, and a PMI certified OPM3 consultant. He is the president of the South India section of AACE International and the convenor of the Indian Project Management Forum. His website is www.xtraplus.co.in

Jim Sloane, PMP, CM, OPM3® Consultant, is owner and founder of Project Management Explorations. He has significant experience as an

engineer, team lead, and project lead in product development environments. Jim has been a consultant and trainer since 1998 with experience
across many industries, including biopharmaceuticals, medical devices,
IT, aerospace, construction products, and telecom. He is an earned value
management (EVM) consultant who focuses on Department of Defense
EVM consulting engagements supporting government reviews and control account manager mentoring. He is a core team member on PMI's
OPM Community of Practice.

▌ CONTENTS

5 Executive Imperatives: The Role of Project Sponsorship in Organizational Success   73

Randall Englund

6 Successful Business Transformation   93

Folake Dosunmu, PMP, PgMP, OPM3

▌ EDITOR'S PREFACE

Rosemary Hossenlopp, PMP

Project management is the bridge between what an organization is and what it needs to become. Organizations continually grapple with how to face the economic, financial, and political challenges that assail their markets, corporate missions, and operational methods. In response to these challenges, project managers are daily tasked with work that enables organizations to build new capabilities in the midst of chaotic conditions and to create the outcomes needed for the future.

The project management bridge is straining under the weight of the mandate for change. Why is it almost buckling? After all, the bridge was built wisely:

- It was built based on historical project management practices for how to get work done.
- It was reinforced with domain-specific wisdom—quality approaches or product development methodologies.
- It has large girder beams that connect it to a stable foundation: project portfolio management.

Yet while this bridge still can carry traffic, it can't support the emerging requirements of the current storm. According to James Conner, director of engineering and technology, UC Berkeley Extension, "Using classical project management, you can successfully fabricate a bridge. But your competitor's strategic use of organization-based project management will create a global powerhouse respected by all."

The terms *organizational project management* and *strategy* are seldom used in the same sentence. Organizational project management aims to change that. A focus on organizational project management helps organizations coordinate the interfaces between:

- Project management
- Program management
- Portfolio management.

It is also intended to help close the gap between project work and operations or the customer.

Doing the right projects *and* doing the project work right can provide the competitive advantage that enables an organization to become a global powerhouse. This is why a group of project management thought leaders got together to write this book. We work in organizations around the world, and we want to rethink how to make project work count—how to ensure that it delivers business results and outcomes. Cumulatively, we have a couple of hundred years of industry experience, and our expertise spans almost every industry and crosses several continents. The passion that links us is our desire to share trends, thoughts, and case studies about how project management is changing from a standalone domain to an end-to-end business footprint.

We wrote this book for those individuals who fund projects, direct projects, or conduct project work. Readers of this book may be called project sponsors, business leaders, operations managers, executive leaders, senior project managers, program managers, portfolio managers, or project management office (PMO) staff. Regardless of their title, all of these individuals are on the front line of project work, daily facing questions such as: "What must be done to improve business outcomes?" "How do we better align ourselves with corporate strategy?" "Which work is the biggest priority?" "How do we organize the work?"

This book was written to offer answers to these questions. The insights our contributors offer are crucial to senior project managers in their role as front-line liaisons with customers, operations, project sponsors, and senior leadership. The book is organized into four parts:

- **Part I. What Is Organizational Project Management?** Organizational project management (OPM) is an emerging trend that is intended to move project managers away from focusing on project management methods and toward focusing on the outcomes needed by the users of our business solutions. This part provides foundational knowledge to understand organizational project management methods.

- **Part II. Strategic Project Management Concepts.** A key concept underlying OPM is alignment between project work and strategy. Several contributors provide practical guidance on how to overcome challenges in organizational alignment and discuss proven business-leader actions that lead to project success.

- **Part III. Insights for Accelerated Project Execution.** Organizational project management is closely linked to organizational maturity. Several contributors offer advice on how high-performance organizations can respond to environmental factors with transformation projects, conduct assessments, and become sensitive to cultural differences when performing project work across time zones and cultures.

- **Part IV. Closing Thoughts for Leaders.** Project work is not done in isolation; it is part of a business system. The final chapters address all the components that must work together to produce effective business outcomes, not just project outcomes.

Before we dive into the substance of OPM, let's consider some mental adjustments that must be made.

Mistaken Guiding Principles

It might be said that project management is simply common sense on steroids. Or, as contributing author Michael O'Brochta notes, "Project management is about applying common sense with uncommon discipline." When I share this statement with clients across the United States, I usually get some guilty laughs. Throughout this book we highlight mistaken concepts about project management that both hinder our profession and cause us to act unwisely. Therefore, in this book, key project management leaders speak to four project management myths in an effort to move the profession forward.

Myth 1: Project Management Is about Project Managers

The project management profession has undergone significant positive change. It has fixed itself up. The role of the project manager has become far more professional; global standards have been created; certifications can be gained; and assessments are used to measure project management maturity.

After this self-improvement push, project managers were eager to be recognized as valuable contributors to the fabric and structure of viable organizations. They were ready for the proverbial prom. They had new dresses and new tuxedos—but in 2001, the limo company called many project managers to tell them that the global recession meant they no longer had a ride to the ball. Many project managers lost their jobs. Management simply could not afford the overhead costs of that administrative role.

Mental Model Adjustment

Why did project managers experience such a large wave of layoffs? It may be that they have been too focused on processes and not on improving organizational outcomes. They talk about scope, cost, and schedule without considering how the project will deliver strategic value. Project managers can get excited about the tools and techniques and lose sight of the goal to deliver desired organizational improvements. Project managers may be too focused on the art of project management at the expense of desired user outcomes. Figure P-1 shows what the traditional PM focus may have looked like.

Yes, project managers care about users. They gather users' requirements, then ask them to sign off on the project at the end. But do project managers stay awake at night thinking about how to improve business operations or how to deal with challenging scheduling, planning, and managing issues? No; these issues are sometimes considered up front and during deployment,

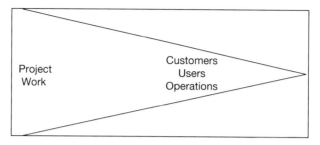

Figure P-1 Traditional Project Management Focus

but then project managers get busy with project management work in the middle of the life cycle.

According to Joseph Sopko, a software and engineering department senior consultant at Siemens Corporate Research, Inc.,

> Project management best practice standards are fairly mature, yet research studies consistently reveal that most organizations fail to realize the benefits that projects were meant to deliver. Why should OPM maturity improvement projects be any different? OPM improvement initiatives are business change programs. If you do not manage benefits, then you will not consistently deliver benefits.
>
> Not everything is best run as a project. What we find is that you can run a project like a program and succeed. However, if you run a program like a project, it's very likely that you will not achieve the benefits intended or be able to sustain them.

What to Read in This Book

How can project managers change? In Chapter 1, Russ McDowell proposes a remedy for our industry. He suggests that we invert our perspective. Figure P-2 shows that we need to keep our eye on delivering benefits to ensure that project management maximizes its impact. McDowell provides a foundation for understanding the meaning and value of organizational project management in changing organizational outcomes. If the focus is first on those we serve, project management will deliver the correct outcomes.

Jim Sloane presents an overview in Chapter 2 of how project managers can shift from simple task execution to strategic focus. Raju Rao, in

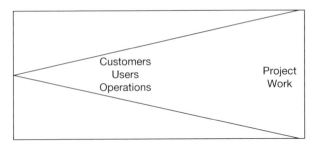

Figure P-2 New Project Management Focus

Chapter 3, presents industry methodologies that can create a stronger linkage between project work and corporate strategic vision.

Myth 2: Project Management Is about Skill Development

Much of the project manager's role can be described by the breadth of project management methodologies, templates, policies, and procedures that govern projectized work. The load of acronyms used in our profession is enough to weary any new (and previously eager) recruit.

Mental Model Adjustment

It is easy to study a project template, learn how to implement it, and increase one's PM skill proficiency. But the future of project management needs more than skill proficiency, it requires leadership. So what is kind of role belongs to the project manager? Is it an influencing role, or a communication and leadership role aimed at delivering organizational improvements? Project managers must be leaders. Project management skills can be taught; leadership can only be inspired.

What to Read in This Book

How can project managers become better leaders? In Chapter 4, Michael O'Brochta challenges business leaders to consider that business success is dependent on project success. According to O'Brochta, the good news is that business leaders can take proven actions that will raise the odds of project success. Randall Englund follows up in Chapter 5 with a discussion of the role of the project sponsor. He suggests ways to change the project environment culture dramatically by improving leadership and the relationship between senior management and project managers.

Myth 3: You Must Improve Project Maturity

Improving project practices is an excellent tactic, but it is narrowly focused on project maturity. There are many global standards regarding how to assess project, product, and initiative maturity, and we are grateful for their contributions—but their usefulness can be limited.

Let's go back to the bridge metaphor. To ensure quality, we can, for example, inspect the nuts and bolts that we installed when we built the bridge. But what happens if the bridge is of high quality but isn't in the correct location? We have wasted organizational assessment resources that could be better used on bridges that do connect critical areas. Assessments often focus on models; organizational project management focuses on linking strategy with project outcome to obtain better business results.

Mental Model Adjustment

Chaotic times dictate a change in focus from project maturity to OPM maturity. We need to view the project environment in terms of linkages to:

- Operations
- Strategy
- Organizational design.

Project managers must be project leaders—business-savvy project professionals who help organizations build the right set of products, services, and results that matter to those we serve.

What to Read in This Book

In Chapter 6, Folake Dosunmu blows the doors off stale thinking with a perspective on project management's role in organizations' transformation efforts. She takes us way beyond the project paradigm of competing demands of cost, time, and scope to understanding how organizations move incrementally through traditional project work to transformative projects that fundamentally change an organization.

Abdur Rafay Badar understands the interactions between organizational culture and strategic alignment. In Chapter 7, he explains how cultural awareness can help companies succeed in project work and even transform themselves. In Chapter 8, Sara Núñez explores the value of performing project environment assessments that deliver organizational improvement. Pavan Kumar Gorakavi analyzes the turnaround of a large public-sector organization in Chapter 9, answering the question of whether OPM concepts can be used in public-service organizations with a resounding yes.

Myth 4: Project Management Is Successful Project Work

Project managers often are considered overhead. Along with thousands of others, I lost my Silicon Valley start-up job in the dot-com crash. The planning, managing, and measuring tasks I performed were delegated instead to the technical team, which was thought to be "really" doing the work.

Why was the work given to the technical team instead of project managers? This is a complex issue, but in part it was due to an industry-wide myopic preoccupation with the profession of project management. Project managers inaccurately believe that the strategic value of coordinating schedules, budgets, and scope is obvious, so they don't emphasize the strategic value and organizational benefits that result from a well-managed project. As a result, project managers present themselves merely as paperwork administrators, and bureaucrats are often cut during recessions.

I consistently hear the following from many of the hundreds of project managers whom I work with around the globe: "All I need to do to be successful is to complete the project work on time, on budget, and within the scope originally defined." This is generally a correct statement; successfully executing a project is the foundation of project management. Unfortunately, many project management professionals have made it the ceiling of their thinking and not the floor from which to build. Organizational project management is much bigger than simply successfully managing project work.

Mental Model Adjustment

OPM is about supporting a business system and its goals. To that end, project managers and top management need to engage in effective communication. Bas de Baar of ProjectShrink.com writes,

> Senior management turns to project management to get things done. Project managers are the Getting-Things-Done-Squad! They drive changes through the thickets and swamps of corporate and global politics, often at dangerously high speeds with zero visibility. There is no time for compliance-for-compliance-sake, review-upon-review, or no-you-cannot-change project management. Any organization performing work project needs leadership and awesome communication.

What to Read in This Book

Marcia Daszko wraps up this book in Chapter 10 by conclusively stating that project management must be part of a larger business system—a system that aligns both strategy and how an organization gets work done. She leaves us with next steps for improving organizational outcomes.

These key voices in Organizational Project Management welcome you into critical conversations about aligning strategy and project work.

▌ ACKNOWLEDGMENTS

I am indebted to my fellow consultants and senior leadership at Management Concepts; to my selfless professional colleagues for their friendship, guidance, and input into my life; and to Myra Strauss and Courtney Chiaparas of Management Concepts for this book's skillful execution.

CHAPTER 1

OPM: Delivering Business Results from Enterprise Strategy

Russ McDowell, PMP

Are you having trouble getting the results you expect from projects you undertake? Do you struggle to decide which initiatives will deliver the best returns or benefits for your organization? Are you trying to take advantage of new opportunities or implement new initiatives in your company but finding that the implementation never seems to go right? Do you need to improve your organization's capacity to respond to today's challenging business environment?

In this chapter, you will discover how you can use organizational project management (OPM) to deliver project results by implementing your enterprise strategies. You will learn:

- How to use proven techniques to implement your organizational strategy—and get tangible results
- How to establish a flexible management approach to capitalize on new opportunities
- About the importance of ensuring each project delivers the business outcomes promised to stakeholders

- Effective ways to ensure the alignment of investments in projects with the strategies of the organization
- How to establish objectivity in the selection and support of projects, based on business criteria.

In today's fast-paced business environment, a company's overall approach to OPM will determine whether it is able to address necessary, critical changes identified in executive management's strategic directions and decisions—and even if the organization will survive.

Most organizations are just in the beginning stages of achieving their strategic objectives through the adoption of project management (PM) best practices. Project managers have their heads down in project work. Executives are buried in bad news. What should we do about this? Start a dialog between project managers and executives on how to deliver benefits, align projects to strategy, and stop wasting time on project work that doesn't matter.

This is OPM. It is the bridge between an organization's strategy and operational outcomes. It is about a real conversation that needs to occur—now!

Whatever You Do, Don't Stand Still!

Today's organizations face many challenges, including:

- The pressure of globalization and new market opportunities
- The need to increase revenues and decrease costs
- The chaos of mergers and acquisitions
- The relentless cry to increase efficiency
- Pressure to reduce time to market for new products
- Downsizing/rightsizing/outsourcing

- The accelerating pace of technology change
- Legislative changes (e.g., the Sarbanes-Oxley Act; banking and financial reporting regulations).

In addition, the recession that began in 2008 has shown that no company or industry is immune to the current turbulence in the market. Pain is everywhere. The spectacular failures of the housing, banking, and automotive industries have provided all too many examples. If your organization is to prosper, it's not enough to stand still. You must adapt quickly to a rapidly changing environment.

Projects, by their nature, are the ideal mechanism for implementing the fast-paced, focused changes that are so necessary to today's business environment. By definition, projects are temporary endeavors, focused on implementing unique solutions while accommodating constraints of resources and scope.

How Can OPM Help?

To understand how OPM can help contribute to the success of your organization, it is first necessary to understand the position that OPM and "projectized activities" play in the day-to-day life of an organization.

First, let's start with a basic definition. According to the Project Management Institute, OPM "is the systematic management of projects, programs, and portfolios in alignment with the organization's strategic business goals."[1] Much of the focus and literature in the field of project management has been on how to ensure that projects are done right. However, the real promise of OPM is not in the proper execution of authorized projects, although this is an important facet. The key to being successful in OPM is to ensure a tight relationship between strategic goals and the implementation of new capabilities.

The Organizational Pyramid

To appreciate what OPM can do for your business, it is important to understand the environment within which it exists. Figure 1-1 illustrates four key components of OPM.

- At the top of the pyramid are the areas traditionally covered by an organization's executive management. This level of management is responsible for the corporate vision—articulating the mission and determining the strategy and objectives that will best attain the vision and mission.

- Below the top level of the pyramid, two approaches that must be balanced for the organization to be successful are shown. On the left side of the pyramid's base is the operations management

Figure 1-1 The Organizational Context of Portfolio Management

of the organization: the day-to-day running of the business, the "keeping the lights on." The focus here is on implementing ongoing, repetitive functions. To compete, organizations tend to optimize for the operation of routine tasks. Thus, the tendency is for this side of the organization to focus on driving the efficiencies of current operations and incrementally improving current functions.

- On the right side of the pyramid are the projectized activities—areas related to project management—including portfolio and program management. Projectized approaches are generally aimed at implementing significant change within an organization.

- The arrows at the bottom of the pyramid, pointing to both recurring operations and projectized activities, indicate that the organization must be supported by a balanced approach to the use of its resources.

The right side of the triangle has been the focus of most of the project management literature. Much has been said, and these multiple voices can help project participants improve the management of projectized activities.

Although PM is important to OPM, it is not our current focus. What no one is talking about is the interfaces and boundaries of operations with the projectized activities. What must happen? Senior management needs more help to optimize the allocation of resources between the operations and the projects. Both aspects require organizational resources (e.g., people, funds, facilities) to perform their roles. Tough decisions are made during high-level operations planning that result in new projects (e.g., setup of new manufacturing lines, upgrades of technology infrastructure, renewal of communications networks).

Doing the Right Projects: The Top of the Pyramid

Henry Ford reportedly said, "The greatest waste in business is doing the wrong thing well." Most organizations have more "good ideas" (i.e., ideas backed by business cases with a positive net present value, alignment to corporate strategy, and a strong cost/benefit ratio) than they have resources to implement. As a result, the executive management is challenged to select the best projects to authorize. (This challenge is addressed by one of the key process groups within the Project Management Institute's *Standard for Portfolio Management*—the "aligning process group.")[2]

At its heart, choosing projects is primarily a business investment decision and should be based on which projects provide the best promise of achieving strategic goals. When making these decisions, it is essential to understand the organization and its objectives and how project deliverables will help the organization achieve its desired business results.

Beginning with the End in Sight: The Bottom of the Pyramid

Organizations do not benefit from undertaking projects! This may seem like heresy in a book on project management, but it is important to realize that projects need to *deliver* something of value to an organization. If you look carefully at Figure 1-1, you will notice that the output of projects is directed toward the ongoing operations. In other words, the results of any project are new or enhanced capabilities for the organization. The organization will achieve benefits from these new capabilities only if the capabilities are actually used in the delivery of services to the clients served by that organization.[3]

Successful OPM requires the transition of key project deliverables at the end of the project. Managers must consider how these deliverables will be used by and affect the operational side of the business. Managers must also consider how the operations team will support the new capabilities delivered by the project throughout the deliverables' life cycle. This life cycle is typically much longer and hence more costly than what it costs to deliver the capabilities through the original project itself.

What Can Outcome Management Do for Me?

Business decisionmakers do not undertake projects for the sake of the deliverables that the project will produce. Good investment decisions are made based on the probability of realizing benefits from that investment. For an organization to realize benefits from a project, it must take the project deliverables (generally, new or improved capabilities or products) and use them—that is, integrate them into operations—to achieve the anticipated benefits. *Outcome management* is defined as "the set of activities for the planning, managing, and realizing of the desired outcomes from initiatives."[4]

Outcomes are different from project deliverables. For example, the deliverable of a project may be a new software product release that is anticipated to achieve a 25 percent increase in market share. The project is complete when the software is released, but the benefits from the new version of the software will be realized only after some period of exposure in the marketplace. Thus, outcome management and benefits realization normally take place outside the context of the project itself. The PRINCE2 project management methodology recognizes this, offering a specified "post-project review plan" that identifies:

- How to measure achievement of expected benefits
- When the various benefits can be measured
- What resources are needed to carry out the review work.[5]

The post-project review is a planned component of the actions that follow project closure. The executives (including the project sponsors and steering committee) are responsible for ensuring that the review happens within the appropriate time frame and that the post-project review plan measures all the benefits specified in the original business case for the project.

Determining whether the intended benefits of the original investment have been delivered allows the organization to close the feedback loop. It provides a metric against which the success of selecting investments in the portfolio can be measured. Thus benefits management is a key component in the management of investments in the project portfolio.

As reported by Public Works and Government Services Canada (PWGSC), a department of the federal government of Canada,

- Benefits realization is the pre-planning for, and ongoing management of benefits promised....
- Sound project management can only enable a business owner (program) to realize intended benefits.
- Accountability for the realization of intended benefits must rest with the business function, not with the IT project.[6]

Outcome management brackets both ends of the traditional project life cycle. On one end is planning for benefits: Before the project has been selected or authorized, the documented business case should indicate the intended benefits that should result from investing in the project. This should include a clear description of how to measure those benefits after the project has finished and its deliverables are put into operational use.

On the other end of the traditional project life cycle, outcome management continues after the project to actually measure and compare attained benefits against planned benefits. Including detailed descriptions and feedback on realized benefits will allow the organization to improve its ability to forecast benefits on future projects and make better investment decisions.

Outcome management through the measurement of benefits resulting from the original investment decision is primarily a business responsibility, not that of project management. It is most likely that the project team will no longer exist when the data become available to do the benefits analysis. As with the original project selection, the measurement of success is done on a business basis, relative to attainment of strategic objectives. The focus on business benefits fosters a higher probability of success on the project itself because it permits senior management to see the direct relationship between an approved investment in a project or program and its intended results. Measuring results and comparing them against anticipated results provides the organization with the necessary feedback to improve its processes for the selection of future investments.

OK, I'm Convinced. How Do I Get Better at OPM?

Most organizations are already performing projects at some level of capability. However, they may not be achieving the success rates they hope for. More important, their investment in projects is not contributing directly to, or meeting expectations for, improvements in the business results. If this is the case, organizations must improve their ability to capitalize on opportunities through the use of projectized activities.

You might be asking, "Are there models out there, or do I need to start from scratch?" While implementing OPM may seem like an intimidating proposition, there are existing approaches to help guide and advance your organization's potential for success. Key components of these approaches are maturity models, such as the *Portfolio, Programme, and Project Management Maturity Model (P3M3)*[7] or the PMI *Organizational Project Management Maturity Model (OPM3®)*.[8] As Figure 1-2 shows, a good maturity model will provide:

- A list of best practices that are accepted in the field being analyzed (in our case, project/program/portfolio management)

- A mechanism for assessing how many of these practices are already in place in an organization (in other words, a method for establishing a baseline)

- A "road map" that shows which areas need improvement and explains how to determine the order in which changes should be implemented.

If you have determined that you want to embark on a journey toward project management improvement, a maturity model suggests a path to follow. Figure 1-3 shows the basic improvement process recommended for organizations following PMI's methodology.

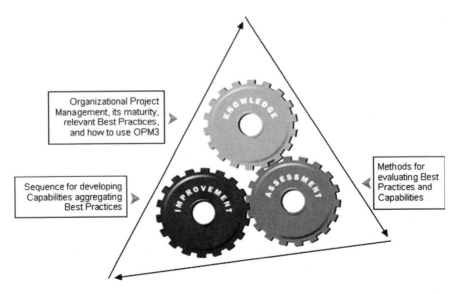

Figure 1-2 Elements of the *Organizational Project Management Maturity Model (OPM3®)*

The better your organization is at implementing projects, the more successfully it will capitalize on strategic changes. Its investments will yield better results. Though this chapter does not detail the steps involved in an OPM3® maturity assessment and improvement cycle, there are some key points your organization should consider when you are trying to improve OPM.

While projectized activities and their related domains (portfolio, program, and project management) are important to OPM, managing these well is not by itself sufficient to ensure success in implementing strategy through projects. To successfully measure and improve your organization's OPM capabilities, you must use a holistic approach, considering other equally important factors.

When you are preparing for an assessment, you must be sure that you understand the organization that you are assessing, particularly its strategic objectives and goals and its business drivers, as well as the environment

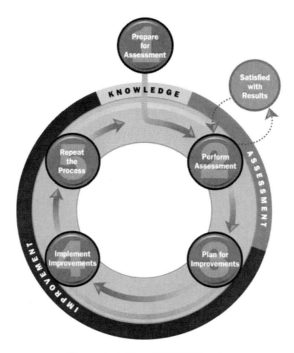

Figure 1-3 The OPM3® Cycle

in which projects are being considered. Is the company led by risk takers? Is it financially driven? Is it seeking a competitive advantage? This stage is represented as "1" in Figure 1-3.

When planning an improvement cycle, it is important to take a baseline measurement. Without a baseline, it is not possible to compare the post-cycle results with the pre-improvement status. Without a basis for comparison, you cannot tell if you have achieved your improvement objectives (or by how much) and if the investment was a good value. Organizational change is a long-term process, and it is important to be able to demonstrate progress and value to senior management.

You must also assess the level of project maturity required to achieve the organization's objectives. Not all organizations need to aim for the highest levels of maturity in projectized activities. Many businesses are more oriented to ongoing operations and only occasionally require projects. Any investment in project maturity should be driven by a clear business case. Organizations already at the requisite level are represented by the "Satisfied with Results" bubble in Figure 1-3.

One of the benefits of basing your improvement process on established standards is that these standards have been developed based on experience in a wide variety of industries, at companies of different sizes, and in geographically and culturally diverse areas. There is value in being able to determine from broader baselines how your company compares with other organizations that are similar in size, are engaged in similar industries, or are in the same geographic area. Using tools such as the OPM3® allows for this comparison against other organizations. Rather than trying to find new solutions to project management challenges that other organizations have solved, use proven techniques; this reduces your risk of failure when implementing new approaches as necessary.

Baby Steps toward OPM

Standard project management and how it differs from regular operations management are well understood, but organizational project management is still in its infancy. Because OPM is relatively new, the literature is not as broad or deep as that on project management, but there are many good references and models that will help guide you. While the improvement process may still seem daunting, I have found through many years of experience in consulting with a wide variety of clients that:

- It is not necessary to develop totally new processes. Build on ones that you already have, and determine the next logical step to improve on them. No one can build a fully mature organization overnight. Start with the key "pain points," and build incrementally. You will realize tangible benefits at each stage of the journey.

- A large investment in some kind of enterprise project management tool set is unnecessary. Most of the time, substantial improvements can be made through simple steps, such as:

  ○ Using common templates/guides for project management documents

  ○ Using checklists in gate reviews to determine if the key points have been addressed so that you can move from one stage to the next on a project/portfolio

  ○ Using spreadsheets to develop portfolio-scoring models, which help ensure that the right projects are selected based on strategic alignment.

Improving an organization's maturity must be done one step at a time. Technology tools by themselves aren't the answer. You must develop an overall integrated approach that includes planned processes and human resources before the benefits of expensive tools will be realized.

Final Thoughts

This chapter has shown why organizational project management is important to business survival in today's environment. While senior executives are able to develop mission statements and strategic goals to address organizational issues, they are finding that it is a challenge to successfully implement organizational initiatives in the face of today's pressures. Many, if not most, strategic initiatives require the organization to make some sort of significant change in the way it is working. It is precisely this type of change that project management best practices have a proven track record of addressing.

The challenge is integrating project management best practices within an organization to achieve the anticipated benefits. Organizational project management offers the required bridge from strategy to operational outcomes. OPM requires a holistic approach to business challenges, the application of best practices when performing projectized activities, and the hand-off/integration of new capabilities to the operations side of the organization. The result is an organization that:

- Invests in project portfolios based on clear, quantified business criteria
- Minimizes risk through the management of investments by applying best practices in project management
- Ensures that the anticipated benefits have been realized through outcome management
- Constantly strives to improve both investment decisions and portfolio oversight through measurement and feedback
- Achieves predictability in running projects
- Has more confidence and better planning capabilities
- Is able to quickly identify, implement, and capitalize on new opportunities
- Has a better success rate of achieving intended results.

An organization with a holistic, mature approach to OPM is an organization able to quickly adapt to new opportunities, respond to external threats, and continue to improve its business management while achieving predictable results. It is, in short, an organization that has a strategic competitive advantage.

Notes

1 Project Management Institute, *Organizational Project Management Maturity Model (OPM3®)*, *Second Edition* (Newtown Square, PA: Project Management Institute, 2008), 9.
2 Project Management Institute, *The Standard for Portfolio Management, Second Edition* (Newtown Square, PA: Project Management Institute, 2008), 37.
3 Office of Government Commerce, Information Technology Infrastructure Library (ITIL), version 3 (London: Office of Government Commerce, 2007).
4 Treasury Board of Canada Secretariat, *Outcome Management Guide and Tools* (Ottawa, ON: Treasury Board of Canada Secretariat, 2006), 6.

5 Office of Government Commerce, *Managing Successful Projects with PRINCE2* (London: Office of Government Commerce, 2005), 365.

6 Treasury Board of Canada Secretariat, "Benefits Realization: Government of Canada Experience," slide 5, presentation to the Organization for Economic Co-operation and Development, February 6, 2006, Paris. Available online at http://www.tbs-sct.gc.ca/emf-cag/outcome-resultat/benefits-avantages/page01-eng.asp (accessed February 1, 2010).

7 Office of Government Commerce, *Portfolio, Programme, and Project Management Maturity Model (P3M3)*, version 1.0 (London: Office of Government Commerce, Feb. 2006).

8 Project Management Institute, *Organizational Project Management Maturity Model (OPM3®), Second Edition* (Newtown Square, PA: Project Management Institute, 2008).

CHAPTER 2

Organizational Alignment: The Intersection of Strategy and Project Work

Jim Sloane, PMP

Are you a business leader who directs or authorizes spending on projects? Do you provide training or mentoring to senior project managers on how to better align projects to strategy? In this chapter, you will discover how linking organizational strategy to project funding will improve your organization's competitive capabilities. You will also learn to select and staff projects with savvy project managers who understand the factors needed to deliver better project outcomes. You will find:

- Guidance on how to align strategy with projects
- Key factors that ensure alignment
- Practical actions project managers can take to improve alignment.

Organizations want their project portfolios to deliver organizational benefits such as:

- Reversal of negative sales trends
- Revenue growth in all markets
- Improvement of the organization's reputation with customers and suppliers

- Restoration of competitive advantage
- Risk-/investment-balanced infrastructure.

The critical question is, what is needed, or what change must take place, to predictably deliver those benefits? My 30 years' experience in commercial and government environments as a manager, engineer, and management consultant has taught me the answer is organizational alignment.

Defining Organizational Alignment

Organizational alignment is the development of consistent models, methods, and communications that allow your project staff to accelerate strategic goals while accomplishing the goals and objectives of the projectized organization. Elements of organizational alignment may include:

- Models of business strategies that provide a viable path to organizational success
- Methods to accomplish the business-unit objectives of the business model strategies through:
  - Change management
  - People
  - Processes
  - Technology
- Communications for the alignment of staff talent and motivation to implement those models and methods.

Organizational alignment between projects and operations is an imperative for companies trying to survive the ever-accelerating changes and increased competition in the business world. As a business leader, you can create an environment in which project results match strategic objectives and accelerate the delivery of organizational benefits. Doing so requires:

- Selecting and controlling projects that further the organization's strategic objectives

- Understanding the changing role of the project manager (PM)
- Relinquishing power to project managers.

All three elements are necessary for any type of organization to remain competitive.

Organizational Alignment Practices in Industry

I work and talk with many executives in the aerospace and high-tech industries. These industries don't have consistent processes, procedures, or plans to describe how they plan, track, or verify projects' delivery of benefits or capabilities to operations or to their customers. Without tracking, adjusting, and verifying project outcomes to maintain alignment with strategic objectives, projects may follow *any* path to completion.

However, some executives are moving away from this traditional ad hoc approach because it is too costly. To stay competitive, organizations must strategically control project outcomes. Here, I share two case studies in which projects, through programs, were aligned to strategic objectives.

One aerospace executive drives alignment of project and organizational strategy through a model of program management. While projects aggregate to programs in this organization, the organization views programs as its strategic initiatives. Therefore, program managers are responsible for delivering benefits to the company. This model is reinforced through several methods, including measuring program managers on the following organizational performance goals:

- Profit
- Return on investment (ROI) capital
- Neutral cash flow
- Value added to the customer (visible via award-fee scores on cost-plus award fee contracts)

- Program performance metrics on contracts and contractor performance assessment reports

- HR goals, such as diversity maturity model scores (e.g., the percentage of female and minority employees) and new graduates hired.

The importance of these performance goals is underscored by a monthly review. Talent management and motivation, or making sure you have the right people for the right job, is focused on these goals; program managers' annual bonuses are tied to achieving the organization's performance goals, which are strategically linked to the division portfolio and the corporate strategy and objectives established by the CEO.

At a broadly diversified multinational company, executive management tasked the company's organizational project management (OPM) director with establishing a corporate business improvement program. The initiative's goals were to assess the alignment between projects and organizational benefits and to establish tracking of benefits. This initiative established several key methods for doing so:

- Standardized language

- Use of benefits profiles

- Blueprints of the goal state

- Program-level governance processes

- Identification of specific business changes that will effect project benefits.

Creating a benefits profile was key to ensuring that projects actually deliver benefits. A *benefits profile* defines the benefit, explains how or where the benefit will be observed, identifies the business unit affected by the program and the indicators or triggers showing that the benefit has been realized, and includes metrics for measuring the benefit realization. Benefit profiles may also indicate who owns the benefit and may list the project dependencies.

At the multinational company, divisional project or program management offices governance enabled and supported planning, executing, and controlling project work in a consistent manner across all projects. This effort was effective in getting buy-in from the organization's division leaders, who were normally suspicious of corporate programs. When the improvement initiative was represented as a divisional program, resistance decreased. This organization used several methods and "evangelized" its messages to optimize its organizational models.

These two examples represent leading-edge organizational models that align strategy to projects. But what does the literature say about organizational project management?

Management Literature Review

I reviewed 13 well-known management books on competitive strategy, business strategy, project management, selling project management to executives, executing strategy, and the project environment. (See the bibliography at the end of this chapter for a comprehensive list of books reviewed.) These books provided significant insight into three key elements:

- Organizational strategy
- Competitiveness as a benefit
- Projects as change initiatives.

All of these are important topics, but the books I reviewed generally discuss each one in isolation. Equally disappointing is that many of these books never make the connection between projects and strategy. Therefore, this chapter suggests methods that ensure alignment between project work and organizational strategy.

Working toward Organizational Alignment

Strategic or organizational alignment is the process of linking business improvement strategy with corporate vision, goals, objectives, and strategy.

Projects transform the strategies into operational improvements in the organization. Projects and strategy must align for an organization to achieve and maintain strategic competitive advantage.

Portfolio Management

Portfolio management is an essential part of corporate strategy. A prolific strategy author, Michael E. Porter, has written much about strategy and its importance for competitive advantage. When business-unit growth strategies begin to conflict with each other, portfolio management is needed to exploit those interrelationships.[1]

According to Porter, the success of an organization's competitive strategy rests on performing unique projects that transform the business. In today's business world, competitive strategy is all about being different and doing activities that bring value to customers in a unique way. Companies that find their niche have greater competitive success, particularly if they are first in the niche.

This is great wisdom. Yet it falls short. Porter does not talk about how projects deliver this "difference." In fact, in three Porter books I studied, *On Competition, Competitive Strategy: Techniques for Analyzing Industries and Competitors*, and *The Competitive Advantage: Creating and Sustaining Superior Performance*, the terms *project* and *project management* are never mentioned![2]

Morgan, Levitt, and Malek discuss alignment of projects with strategy—specifically, how a portfolio process can benefit all projects.[3] Projects can be broken into three broad categories—those that:

- *Work in the business; deliver products using existing processes.* Routine, day-to-day projects that an organization must do to continue serving its mission fall into this category. A portfolio process can determine which of these projects are most beneficial and ensure organizational alignment.

- ***Work on the business; improve business processes.*** These projects are funded to optimize either project or operations processes. Projects in this category compete for funding and human resources; portfolio processes can be used to determine which projects will deliver the greatest benefits.

- ***Transform the business.*** This category consists of strategic initiatives driven by projects that change the business. These projects are high-risk and high-reward. They can also be governed by a portfolio process that manages competing factors of risk and reward.[4]

The portfolio process is predominantly driven by portfolio governance, which requires sponsorship or supervision to keep the portfolio relevant and functioning by making timely decisions about changes to the portfolio. Project selection is also a part of the portfolio process. The portfolio sponsor evaluates, prioritizes, selects, and assigns performance metrics to each potential project based on its ability to support strategic objectives. Choosing the right projects is a large part of the sponsorship challenge. The projects are tracked to verify whether the expected benefits are realized.

Morgan, Levitt, and Malek write that, in addition to portfolio processes, all types of projects can be helped by the following initiatives:

- Program and project closure processes
- Technical change approval processes
- Change review, using portfolio processes for decision-making
- Sponsorship training
- Decision-making processes that support right decisions versus decision rights
- Benefits tracking systems
- Collecting, managing, and distributing the knowledge captured from completed projects

- Program and project manager reward systems (which must be converted from output to outcome metrics)
- Design-review and stage-gate processes, including outcome analysis requirements.[5]

Project Methodologies

Kerzner suggests that a project management methodology is key to achieving strategic objectives because it provides consistency of initiatives across the organization, raising its overall capabilities.[6] He also suggests that the larger and more complex the organization, the more difficult alignment becomes.

What happens without a methodology that is supported and enforced across the organization? Projects may drift toward the agendas and goals of their own team or management. If project sponsors are left to their own agendas, project goals frequently parallel the (possibly short-sighted) goals of the sponsor. Many sponsors are compensated for quarterly stock performance, not strategic objectives or specific project objectives.

The Project Management Office

Harvey A. Levine, a longtime project management consultant and PMI fellow, agrees with Kerzner.[7] Levine goes a little further, suggesting that a project or program management office (PMO) facilitates the collection and use of project selection and decision-making data. Levine also suggests that a portfolio governance team is needed. This team would direct the categorization, evaluation, selection, prioritization, and balancing of projects in the portfolio. It would also monitor and control the risk associated with portfolio projects.

The Key Project Manager Mindset

Merging project success with strategy wasn't discussed much until the late 1990s; soon after, various scholars and practitioners began writing about it.[8]

Cohen and Graham really dug into it in their book *The Project Manager's MBA: How to Translate Project Decisions into Business Success.*[9] What mindset is needed for project managers to succeed? Project managers must focus on contributing to organizational strategy by ensuring that projects they work on increase business value. There must be a bottom-line benefit to project work.

Improving Alignment

A project manager can boost his or her ability to contribute to business results by focusing on the following:

- Business results processes
- Finance basics
- Marketing and the business systems approach
- "Thought experiments," in which the project manager acts as an entrepreneur in a venture.

Business Results Processes

In *The Project Manager's MBA*, Cohen and Graham write, "Our belief is that the standard way of interconnecting the business perspective of upper management with the technical and tactical perspective of the project team and project manager is outmoded."[10] Project managers are increasingly realizing they are part of a *business* process, not a technical process. This is definitely a change in perspective for the PM, who in the past was responsible for being a technical leader first, business leader second. PMs must understand the difference between business and technical leadership and embrace the idea of being a business leader first, then a technical PM. Projects can provide a strategic competitive advantage; the PM must recognize this and treat them accordingly.

Relinquishing executive power to project managers is a key message. If upper managers are competition-savvy, they will allow PMs to take on this new role, which includes accountability for delivering the project benefits to the organization's operations. Becoming a business leader is a big increase in responsibility for the PM—it may include selling the product, delivering a new service, or spinning off a new business unit. The bottom line is that "the PM needs to think more like a CEO of a small enterprise, and upper management needs to think more like a PM so they can master the technical knowledge that drives projects."[11] Levine calls this broader perspective that encompasses more than just the project life cycle the *project portfolio life span.*[12]

Finance Basics

PMs must understand the basics of finance and accounting to understand the "business of business," particularly the impacts of cash flow and cash cycle on the enterprise, and must learn how to contribute to creating economic value. Once PMs grasp the concepts of business finance, they will be trusted to make decisions about project budget allocations. They also can look for opportunities and will be able to take advantage of them—a new responsibility for many PMs. Cohen and Graham advise project managers to understand and use business concepts to enable greater control over project budgets:

> Understanding and using business concepts about costs for project decision making is the only way that project managers will escape the tyranny of the budget. In the past the project manager was often hobbled with a budget that focused on minimizing costs, often stifling creativity and effective decision making. This was done because upper managers did not believe the project managers could make decisions in the best interest of the organization.[13]

Project managers rarely think in business terms, but they must begin to do so. This business knowledge will make PMs part of the strategic competitive advantage. We suggest that PMs become familiar now with how their business finances its initiatives, from borrowing through investing to operating, paying off debt, and providing return on investment to investors. To do this, PMs must develop a working knowledge of two financial reports: the balance sheet and the income statement.

Marketing and the Business Systems Approach

Project managers need to know a lot about the market their company is involved with. In the past, marketing was thought of as a nebulous concept, like sales, and it was not the focus of project managers trying to produce a final product. Rewards were based on product delivery; sometimes product delivery was based on internal assumptions about what would sell instead of on a customer- or market-centric philosophy.[14] Cohen and Graham believe an understanding of the market will work to a project manager's advantage:

> [Understanding] the processes of marketing increase[s] the project manager's ability to craft a project outcome that solves customer problems better than the competition's product can. If this can be done, the final outcome will have the competitive advantage, and that advantage will increase the potential for sales or use of that outcome.[15]

A project manager who is in touch with his or her market and interacts with it to discover customer needs will be a more effective business partner to upper management. It is important for PMs, if they are to become business partners, to understand and work in business systems. Cohen and Graham explain that this means understanding how a project fits in the organizational strategy and how its success or failure would affect the business.[16] Familiarity with business systems enables the PM to walk, talk, and think like a CEO of a start-up.

The PM-as-CEO concept, however, does not seem to have made its way from the "C suite" to "Main Street" projects yet. My experiences consulting and teaching project managers at many Silicon Valley companies has shown that most PMs are still unaware that they can take on these business-minded responsibilities. I always ask students in my project management classes if they are responsible for project budgets, and in every class, at least half of them say no. This tells me we have a long way to go before we become really smart, worldwide competitors by entrusting cost management—let alone ROI—to project managers.

Thought Experiments

The "thought experiment" discussed in *The Project Manager's MBA* is a way of viewing projects as company ventures—potential businesses that someone might invest in to realize some return.[17] Each company venture has a project team and a project outcome life cycle (POL) team. These teams are responsible for the original business case, through sales to the market and return on investment. Their managers' bonus compensation depends on the financial success of the project, not on broader business results that affect the company as a whole. This changes how the managers and team members perform their roles:

- Project leaders view budgets as solutions, not constraints, and they intelligently trade off costs and customer satisfaction.

- Managers responsible for the project managers view the projects as supporting their goals and compensation, motivating them to provide project return on investment.

- Venture core teams—the essential part of the project team—must include people from each link in the value chain that serves customers, including suppliers and intermediary customers.

- Project outcome life cycle (POL) team representatives must also be on the venture project core team to provide input during project initiation, planning, and execution. They can help keep the project aligned with the expected organizational benefits.

- The project team hands off the project to the POL team to implement the project deliverables in the organization. The POL compares business results to stated project expectations.

Taking Action Today

Project decisions should always be made with the end deliverable and competing demands—scope, cost, schedule, quality, customer satisfaction, and benefits delivered to ongoing operations—in mind. But most companies don't yet see their projects this way. So what can project managers do right now to prepare for the expanded role they must play to be part of a competitive business? Here are six straightforward steps they can take immediately:

1. Develop a business case for every project. The business case should state the source of the numbers for price, sales volume, and production and operating costs. Tailor a business case template for your organization.

2. Think strategically, viewing your project as part of the larger scheme of the organization and the value chain. You should be able to describe the business environment, be familiar with the market and market strategy the project supports, and understand how the project sustains the competitive advantage of the organization and how other projects support the company strategy. Be able to explain how this project will help implement the organizational strategy, and link the numbers to that strategy using a balanced scorecard or a similar planning and management tool.

3. Convert the business plan to a project management plan and use it to guide project execution.

4. Use the list of stated benefits to plan, execute, and control the project.

5. Ensure a smooth transition to the business unit operations by forming a benefit implementation team.

6. Track the POL and evaluate performance based on outcome metrics established during planning.

This six-step process will help businesses and projects managers develop a process to ensure that organizational benefits are realized from projects.

Working toward Alignment

I was struck by the dearth of recent information on the strategic aligning of projects and business operations to achieve a competitive advantage. As we move forward, emphasizing the strategic alignment of projects will help us all learn and circulate much more information on the subject.

At this time, however, most companies have not made efforts to align their projects with corporate strategy. We have listed clear and definitive actions PMs can take now to improve the alignment in their organizations. These actions may not be fully implemented as standard processes until upper management changes its view from thinking of project management as a tactical initiative to accepting projects as strategic activities. Many executives are still in learning mode and will adopt management techniques that promote competitive advantage as they gain experience. It is as difficult for executives to shift their thinking as it is for PMs to act like business partners. Upper management can make an effort by:

- Allowing PMs to engage in the thought experiment—as entrepreneurs in a company venture that someone might invest in to realize some return
- Striving to understand projects' technical aspects
- Participating in training on the value of project strategic alignment.

Project managers have some learning to do as well. They should:

- Learn finance and accounting
- Take responsibility for project outcomes
- Embrace the concept of delivering outcomes and benefits
- Think about the strategic value of a project when making any decisions: Does the project support organizational objectives? Which ones?

- Incorporate project value language—that is, the explanations given for benefit expectations—in the appropriate project initiation, planning, execution, control, and closing processes and documentation. At a minimum, this language should appear in the:
  - Business case
  - Charter
  - Requirements
  - Project plan
  - Quality assurance and control metrics
  - Project team training
  - Stakeholder management plan
  - Project knowledge capture (lessons learned)
  - Procurement processes
  - Closing processes.

The Wisdom of Alignment

While attending the Project Management Institute Global Congress, North America, in October 2009, I followed the organizational project management track and heard the same statements over and over:

- A PMO, whether managing portfolios, programs, or projects, or a system of PMOs, is essential to the success of strategic alignment.
- Portfolio management as a discipline is a must.
- An organization must have a portfolio governance body.
- Provide a business case that describes in detail how the project supports organizational objectives for at least the high-priority, high-risk projects.
- Be patient. Change requires a lot of work and time to take effect in organizations that are trying to become more competitive.

- Future projects will be much more successful if they are aligned with strategy and their alignment is verified periodically.
- Project managers will become better business partners if they embrace their new role as "CEO" of their projects.
- Executive management can increase their organizations' value if they embrace project managers as business partners—a win-win-win for business.

Next Steps

How can we ensure that projects align with our strategic objectives?

- Train project managers to be CEOs of small enterprises, and hire PMs with MBAs.
- Incorporate the organizational strategic objectives that the project supports into the project documentation in the business case, project plan, and charter, at a minimum.
- Establish an implementation team that is responsible for tracking the project and ensuring it delivers the benefits expected.
- Set up a PMO.
- Set up a governance board.

Bibliography

Cohen, Dennis J., and Robert J. Graham. *The Project Manager's MBA: How to Translate Project Decisions into Business Success*. Hoboken, NJ: John Wiley & Sons, Inc., 2001.

Dvir, Dov, Dragan Milosevic, Aaron J. Shenhar, and Hans Thamhain. *Linking Project Management to Business Strategy*. Newtown Square, PA: Project Management Institute, 2007.

Graham, Robert J., and Randall L. Englund. *Creating an Environment for Successful Projects*, 2nd ed. San Francisco: Jossey-Bass, 2003.

Kaplan, Robert S., and David P. Norton. *Alignment: Using the Balanced Scorecard to Create Corporate Synergies*. Boston: Harvard Business School Press, 2003.

————. *The Balanced Scorecard: Translating Strategy into Action*. Boston: Harvard Business School Press, 1996.

Kerzner, Harold. *Applied Project Management: Best Practices on Implementation*. Hoboken, NJ: John Wiley & Sons, Inc., 2000.

Levine, Harvey A. *Project Portfolio Management*. San Francisco: Jossey-Bass, 2005.

Morgan, Mark, Raymond Levitt, and Elliot Malek. *Executing Your Strategy: How to Break It Down and Get It Done*. Boston: Harvard Business School Press, 2007.

Morris, Peter, and Ashley Jamieson. *Translating Corporate Strategy into Project Strategy: Realizing Corporate Strategy through Project Management*. Newtown Square, PA: Project Management Institute, 2004.

Pennypacker, James, and San Retna. *Project Portfolio Management: A View from the Management Trenches*. Hoboken, NJ: John Wiley & Sons, Inc., 2009.

Pfeffer, Jeffrey, and Robert I. Sutton. *The Knowing-Doing Gap: How Smart Companies Turn Knowledge into Action*. Boston: Harvard Business School Press, 2000.

Porter, Michael E. *On competition*. Boston: Harvard Business School Press, 2008.

————. *Competitive Strategy: Techniques for Analyzing Industries and Competitors*. New York: Free Press, 1998.

————. *Competitive Advantage: Creating and Sustaining Superior Performance*. New York: Free Press, 1985.

Notes

1 Michael E. Porter, *Competitive Advantage: Creating and Sustaining Superior Performance* (New York: Free Press, 1985), 318 and 320.

2 Michael E. Porter, *On Competition* (Boston: Harvard Business School Press, 2008); *Competitive Strategy: Techniques for Analyzing Industries and Competitors* (New York: Free Press, 1998); and *Competitive Advantage: Creating and Sustaining Superior Performance* (New York: Free Press, 1985).

3 Mark Morgan, Raymond Levitt, and Elliot Malek, *Executing Your Strategy: How to Break It Down and Get It Done* (Boston: Harvard Business School Press, 2007), 14.

4 Ibid.

5 Ibid., 235.

6   Harold Kerzner, *Applied Project Management: Best Practices on Implementation* (New York: John Wiley & Sons, Inc., 2000), 101–103.

7   Harvey A. Levine, *Project Portfolio Management* (San Francisco: Jossey-Bass, 2005), xiv.

8   See for example Robert J. Graham and Randall L. Englund, *Creating an Environment for Successful Projects, Second Edition* (San Francisco: Jossey-Bass, 2003), and Dennis J. Cohen and Robert J. Graham, *The Project Manager's MBA: How to Translate Project Decisions into Business Success* (Hoboken, NJ: John Wiley & Sons, Inc., 2001).

9   Dennis J. Cohen and Robert J. Graham, *The Project Manager's MBA: How to Translate Project Decisions into Business Success* (Hoboken, NJ: John Wiley & Sons, Inc., 2001).

10 Ibid., xii.

11 Ibid., xii.

12 Harvey A. Levine, *Project Portfolio Management* (San Francisco: Jossey-Bass, 2005), xiii.

13 Dennis J. Cohen and Robert J. Graham, *The Project Manager's MBA: How to Translate Project Decisions into Business Success* (Hoboken, NJ: John Wiley & Sons, Inc., 2001), 136.

14 Ibid., 109–110.

15 Ibid., 111.

16 Ibid., 58–59.

17 Ibid., 199.

CHAPTER 3

How to Align Project Work with Strategic Vision

Raju Rao

What methods, tools, and techniques can senior leaders use to align strategy with projects? What industry best practices can you leverage in your organization? How can teams balance the need to focus on frameworks for alignment with people-oriented issues and challenges? These are key questions for corporate leaders and senior project management professionals who need to improve their project results.

This chapter explores successful techniques for aligning project work with organizational strategy. Specifically, the chapter:

- Provides a practical definition of aligning strategy with project work
- Explains why it so difficult to align strategy and projects
- Describes critical alignment metrics
- Explores various approaches to aligning strategy and projects
- Reviews various models and frameworks for and case studies on alignment
- Helps the reader appreciate the relevance of the human factor in the alignment process.

In the last several years, a lot of research activity has been directed toward understanding the relationship between strategy and projects. Many of these research reports have emphasized the importance of aligning strategy and projects and the benefits of alignment, but very little research has been devoted to *how* to make this happen.[1] Fortunately, many organizations have developed practices and processes to relate project output to strategic vision.

Defining Alignment

Alignment is the correct positioning of components in relation to each other. In an organization, it means continually adjusting the direction of an initiative to achieve objectives. More simply, it means connecting what you *intend to achieve* to what you are *doing*.[2] The intent of alignment is to reflect at the operational level what is expected in the boardroom. Strategic vision is put into action; dreams are converted into reality.

In effect, this alignment from strategic vision to operational reality happens under constraints, such as:

- A timeline specified by the customer or required by market or regulatory bodies
- Available human, financial, and material resources
- Differing stakeholder needs and expectations
- External factors, such as market forces and government regulations.

Because of the challenges posed by these constraints, the interaction between strategic vision and operational action has to be continually managed.

A common metaphor used to understand teamwork, leadership, and alignment compares these concepts to the migratory flight patterns and behavior of geese. What lessons can geese teach project managers? Consider the following facts:

- *Fact:* The "V" formation in which geese fly allows them to travel 70 percent farther than they would out of formation. They expend less effort—or, rather, are able to do more with the same effort, which is what organizations are setting out to do.
  - *Key question:* How good is your **resource optimization** process?
- *Fact:* Whenever a goose falls out of formation, it quickly gets back into formation to take advantage of the lifting power of the bird immediately in front. When a goose gets sick, wounded, or shot down, two geese drop out of formation and follow it down to help protect it.
  - *Key question:* How **cooperative** are your teams?
- *Fact:* When the lead goose gets tired, it rotates back into formation and another goose rotates in to fly at the point position.
  - *Key question:* What is your organization's **commitment** to shared leadership?

How does a flock of geese maintain continual alignment in flight? It does so through culture, cooperation, and commitment—which we'll discuss relative to project management later in this chapter.

Critical Alignment Factors

While geese are naturally able to align themselves to a shared culture and to cooperate and commit to a goal, many organizations find this shared culture, cooperation, and commitment elusive. Geese are more fortunate; they deal with less complexity. They are not burdened with humans' behavioral issues. In organizations, in spite of good risk management and solid business cases, life happens and things change.

Projects, no matter how well mapped out, can drift away from corporate strategy.[3] Why does this happen? What issues and challenges do organizations face when aligning projects and strategy?

- Projects are implemented under dynamic situations and are constantly changing, due to customer requirements, market forces, political changes, government regulations, technology, and strategic shifts in the organization itself.
- Human behavior is variable and unpredictable.
- Globalization, technology, and different organizational structures, such as open source and networks, have made the business world more complex.

These challenges fall into two categories: constraints and issues (see Figure 3-1). Among these, people-related issues may be the most significant of the challenges. They are difficult to address and the least understood. When working to align projects with strategy, we should employ analytical techniques; establish a human approach that resonates with the people who make up an organization; and understand the strategic value of projects.

Employing Analytical Techniques

Organizations must measure performance and develop improvement benchmarks. Using metrics can bridge the gap between desired performance

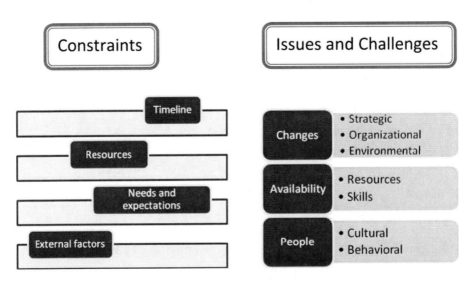

Figure 3-1 Constraints and Issues Affecting Organizational Alignment

and current performance. *Strategic metrics*, which include financial returns, growth rates, and technical assessments, track the business objectives of the organization, taking into account the complexity of the marketplace and the external environment. *Operational* or *project metrics* track tactical objectives to manage performance at the project, program, and portfolio levels of an organization. Examples include timelines and metrics that assess cost or resource optimization, risk, and scope.

The measures used to assess performance at the strategic level are different from those used at the operational or project level. Many organizations find it difficult to relate the different types of metrics, primarily because these organizations do not have an infrastructure that enables them to measure appropriate metrics at different levels of the organization.

Two ways to develop an organizational infrastructure conducive to collecting metrics are 1) to consider which evaluative data would give the most pertinent information about a particular industry or domain based on its work practices and technology and 2) to encourage reciprocal awareness by senior executives and operational staff of the other's work and objectives. In other words, senior executives must be sensitive to operational-level issues, and those working at the operational level need to be educated about strategic goals and thinking.

This second point is a matter of communication and awareness. Senior executives can conduct informal meetings with operational staff, who themselves should be afforded an opportunity to attend seminars and continuing education programs to understand executive conceptual frameworks and objectives.

Key question: Does your organization use processes or methods to relate strategic and operational or project metrics among divisions/ business units within the organization?

Establishing a Human Approach

Humans are affected, positively and negatively, by emotional factors. When working in organizations and as part of a team, we subjugate our individual interests and aspirations to attend to larger objectives. Often, this subjugation goes against our spirit of individualism and free thinking. This makes the process of alignment more complex. We must proactively work on solutions with a human approach. Cooperation helps us arrive at win-win solutions when we must put aside our own inclinations or motivations for the good of the team or the organization.

> **Key question: How well does your organization use cooperation as a means to achieve alignment?**

Understanding the Strategic Value of Projects

When there is a gap between an organization's current performance and where it strives to go, it initiates projects. A survey conducted by Price-waterhouseCoopers in Europe established that operational initiatives like strategic planning, capital budgeting, and organizational change are all executed through projects. Therefore, project management is a key strategic tool to drive these initiatives, and those organizations that understand its importance will outperform the competition.[4]

Only some organizations understand the strategic value of project work and explicitly connect corporate and business-unit strategy to project strategy. Most organizations do not take project work into account when formulating processes for strategy implementation.[5] In these organizations, an understanding of the strategic dimension of projects is missing, and project management is perceived "only" as a tool and technique for operational execution.[6] But many corporate initiatives are in fact projects and will benefit if PM practices and processes are applied to them. Better alignment between strategy and projects will require a change to the perception that project management is only a tactical discipline.

> Key question: Does your organization acknowledge the value of project work in accomplishing organizational goals?

Projects, Programs, and Portfolios

Organizational project management (OPM) is the alignment of an organization's projects, programs, and portfolios (PPP) with its overarching strategy. Projects are generally individual work streams, programs manage multiple work streams, and portfolios comprise the processes of selecting and governing projects and programs in an optimized way. Many project management standards, books, literature, and organizations advocate viewing project work through the perspective of these project/program/portfolio categories. Examples include the Project Management Institute's *Organizational Project Management Maturity Model* (OPM3®), the International Project Management Association's IPMA Competence Baseline, and the Project Management Association of Japan's P2M, among others.

The PPP framework can be applied to most government, commercial, or nonprofit organizations. This concept can even be applied on a national level.[7] Similarly, using the concept of projects, programs, and portfolios, a nation can be managed similarly to an organization to achieve its long-term strategic vision.

> Key question: Does your organization use organizational project management processes?

Project Portfolio Management

Project portfolio management (PPM) is another key tool for aligning strategy with projects. Key PPM techniques include project or program reporting and, more importantly for our discussion, making recommendations on aligning and optimizing projects or processes. More attention has been given to this practice in the last few years. Some sectors are more proactive in applying PPM—for instance, in the pharmaceutical industry, where product development projects are of strategic importance.

A number of PPM tools are available to facilitate organizations' alignment initiatives.[8] These tools can be used to perform project portfolio analysis, develop proposals for realignment and optimization with regard to strategic goals, and build governance and decision-making processes into the project portfolio.

> **Key question: How rigorous are the project portfolio techniques your organization uses to select projects or programs?**

Information Technology

Information technology can provide significant support to alignment efforts, particularly in large organizations and for global initiatives. High-performing organizations employ the following best practices when using IT tools and systems to align strategy and projects:

- Integrate strategy execution management, portfolio management, program/project management, and performance management functions
- Develop alternative strategic and project portfolio scenarios structure
- Provide information to senior management on the availability of project resources
- Provide the capability to monitor and control risks, issues, and financials across portfolios
- Enable appropriate communication of strategy and strategic performance throughout the strategic management chain, both top to bottom and bottom to top.[9]

> **Key question: Does your organization use IT tools and systems to align strategy and projects?**

Alignment Models and Frameworks

Organizations can use a number of models and frameworks to relate business objectives to project objectives (see Figure 3-2). Some organizations proactively and explicitly relate strategy and projects using these methods; others do not.

Model or Framework	Features
Why-how framework	Lists objectives at policy, strategic, and operational levels; facilitates vertical and horizontal analysis; also called ends-means framework[10]
Logical frame (logframe) approach	Used to identify the hierarchy of objectives and core assumptions about the project process. Results in a logframe matrix document that connects project elements.[11]
Military mission and means framework	Organizes project elements into seven levels—the highest level is purpose or mission; the lowest level is interactions or effects.[12]
Business motivation model	Used to relate the elements of a business plan and the factors influencing it: vision, goals, objectives, mission, strategies/tactics, and influences.[13]
Profiling management (P2M)	Clarifies project ambiguity by establishing the who, what, when, why, where, which, and how of a project.[14]
Goal-question-metric (GQM) template	Measurement model that defines project goals, questions, metrics.[15]
Hoshin planning	Management process that addresses key elements of business management: vision, policy development, policy deployment, and policy control; linked to total quality management.[16]

Figure 3-2 Common Alignment Methods

Why-How Framework

Youker and Brown (2001) devised a *why-how framework* using the concept of hierarchy of objectives to relate measures of outcomes at the policy, strategic, and project levels of an organization.[17] A why-how framework can be used to connect objectives at the portfolio, program, and project levels. In this way, you can translate strategic objectives to operational objectives.

Figure 3-3 illustrates a why-how framework for building a cathedral. Start at the top of the hierarchy and look down to answer the "how" questions; start at the bottom and look up to answer the "why" questions. While vertical logic answers the why-how questions in this example, you could also create a model using horizontal logic to relate measured results to assumptions.[18]

Figure 3-4 shows a why-how framework for a process improvement project. This method can be used for practically any organization or project.

Logical Framework Approach

The logical framework (logframe) approach is a project design methodology developed for the United States Agency for International Development, and

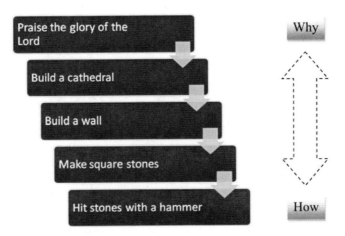

Figure 3-3 Why-How Framework

Reprinted with permission from Robert Youker.[19]

Figure 3-4 Why-How Framework for a Process Improvement Project

it is widely used by many organizations in the development sector, including the World Bank. Developed mainly for infrastructure development projects, it mixes models for strategic planning and management by objectives. The logframe approach can help organizations identify the hierarchy of objectives, measures of each objective, and core assumptions about the project process.

Development of the logframe approach consists of the following steps:

- Analysis: Problem tree, objective tree, and alternatives
- Formulation: Objectives and assumptions
- Identification: Assessment indicators and means of verification.

The result of this exercise is a logframe—a document that connects a project's goal, purpose, output, and activities with indicators of achievement, means of verification, risks, and assumptions in a matrix format.

Military Mission and Means Framework

As the name suggests, the military mission and means framework was developed by the U.S. Department of Defense for use in the armed forces. It organizes a project into seven groups or levels.

Level 7: Purpose, mission—why?

Level 6: Context, environment—under what circumstances?

Level 5: Index, location/time—where?

Level 4: Tasks, operations—what?

Level 3: Functions, capabilities—how well?

Level 2: Components, forces—by whom?

Level 1: Interactions, effects—what are the conditions?

The levels provide the context to relate the various components of the project with one another.

Business Motivation Model

The business motivation model has been developed in the field of information systems. It is used to relate the elements of a business plan and the factors influencing it:

- *Ends:* The future state the business wants to achieve; the vision/goals/objectives
- *Means:* The methods the business will employ to achieve those ends; the mission/strategy/tactics
- *Influencers:* The things that will shape and impact the business; internal or external influences; strengths, weaknesses, opportunities, and threats; risks or rewards.

The business motivation model is designed to answer two fundamental questions:

- *What* is needed to achieve what the enterprise wishes to achieve?
- *Why* does each element of the business plan exist?

Linking a business motivation model to other modeling techniques, such as business process models and unified modeling language models, helps provide traceability between the business strategy and the processes and systems that implement that strategy.

Profiling Management (P2M)

The P2M standard from Japan is probably the only project management standard that considers project strategy management to be a separate discipline and introduces the concept of *profiling*, which allows organizations to clarify the ambiguity that is so common at the beginning of projects. Profiling establishes the who, what, when, why, where, which, and how of a project.[20]

Goal-Question-Metric (GQM)

The GQM method is used in the software industry. It is a measurement model that defines projects on three levels:

- Conceptual (goal)
- Operational (question)
- Quantitative (metric).

The GQM can be used following these steps:

1. Develop a set of corporate, division, and project business goals and associated measurement goals for productivity and quality.

2. Generate questions (based on models) that define those goals as completely as possible in a quantifiable way.

3. Specify the data that must be collected to answer those questions and to track process and product conformance to the goals.

4. Develop mechanisms for data collection.

5. Collect, validate, and analyze the data in real time to provide feedback to projects for corrective action.

6. Analyze the data postmortem to assess conformance to the goals and to make recommendations for future improvements.

A GQM template can be used to document a project's object of study, purpose, focus, and stakeholders.

Hoshin Planning

The concept of *Hoshin Kanri* originated in Japan and was initially used in the manufacturing industry.[21] *Hoshin* translates to *direction* and *focus*, and *Kanri* translates to *alignment* and *reason*. It has since been successfully deployed in some form by many organizations, including Sundaram Clayton, Toyota, Bank of America, and IBM. Hoshin planning is a management process that roughly encompasses four key elements of business management: vision, policy development, policy deployment, and policy control. It is also directly linked to a fifth: total quality management. Hoshin planning can be used to relate strategic-level initiatives to results at the operating level on an ongoing basis. It is dependent on cooperation and buy-in from the people in the organization to be effective.

Comparing Different Models

We've seen that many models or frameworks are available to use. Which one should you use, and under what circumstances? The manner in which each model or framework is devised in terms of goals and objectives and the metrics used for measuring outcomes vary from one industry to another. Each industry focuses on the information that is relevant and important to it.

To reduce organizational resistance to a method or framework, choose one that is familiar or aligned to your industry. If there is no standard for your industry, the why-how framework is probably the easiest to follow and can be applied to many environments. The why-how framework is generic and has not been developed with a specific domain or industry in mind.

Implementation Challenges

Currently, these methods or frameworks for aligning strategy and projects are not widely used, and they are infrequently mentioned in common project management standards. However, as environmental pressures build up in organizations, those willing to use a framework to align projects and strategies will most likely find more success than those without an alignment method. Figure 3-5 lists alignment methods that have been successfully used in four major industries.[22]

Organizations that have used alignment methods to successfully translate corporate strategy into project strategy tend to have similar project, program, and portfolio management processes and philosophies. These organizations cascade processes from the corporate level down through strategic business units to individual units. This information is typically reported in strategic management literature in terms of objectives, goals, and strategies.

Organizations using alignment methods also tend to recognize the importance of portfolio management and use it to select, not to manage, projects and programs. They rely on program management to monitor business benefits and use business cases as an input in those processes. And they facilitate better communication, accountability, and more successful

Domain	Key Tools, Methodologies, or Practices
Aerospace	Business process models and a structured process.
Financial services	High-level business processes. Management of the front end as a phase that is distinct from implementation. Benefit management emphasized during program management.
Pharmaceutical	Process model dominated by the drug-development process. Dedicated portfolio management process. Asset management or technology platform emphasized during program management. Structured process. Value management principles.
Transportation	Business process models. Budget accountability and responsibility.

Figure 3-5 Effective Use of Alignment Frameworks in Four Industries

implementation by using process aids (e.g., flow charts that show inputs and outputs and describe staff roles and responsibilities.[23]

> **Key question: What method or framework can your organization use as a standard process to relate or align strategy with projects?**

Culture, Communication, and Commitment

The "three Cs"—culture, communication, and commitment—are key to successful project management or operations. However, when an organization is working to align projects and strategy, the three Cs take on a special significance because the organization is in constant flux and an onslaught of information must be managed.

Many organizations have used analytical methods and frameworks with highly rigorous processes to align strategy and project work. But are these analytical approaches good enough? Let us for a moment go back to the story of the geese. To reach their goal, geese rely mostly on soft skills such as cooperation and shared leadership. Your organization's approach should be no different: Alignment methods will be successful only if they are performed with people and soft skills in mind.

Let's consider each of the Cs in turn.

Culture

Some organizations are able to effectively align strategy and projects; others are not. Those that cannot may not be deploying the right methods or frameworks, but culture also has a role to play here. Kotter and Heskett define *culture* as "beliefs, goals and values that guide the behavior of an organization's members."[24]

Organizations that are agile can quickly adjust corporate strategy and portfolio spending priorities and can deliver projects that give value to operations and increase profits. According to Jim Highsmith, *agile organizations* are those that "have the ability to both create and respond to change in order to profit in a turbulent business environment."[25] By comparison, bureaucratic organizations find it difficult to adapt and to maintain the alignment of projects with strategy.

Organizational alignment requires consistency and compatibility between strategic and cultural paths.[26] Values espoused by an organization are largely cultural and are dictated by what its members believe in and do in day-to-day work. Examples of such values could be an openness when dealing with customers or suppliers, an insistence on a high level of quality, or underplaying the commercial aspects of business. Alignment takes place when cultural factors are in sync with strategic goals.

> **Key question: Does your organization support strategic alignment by promoting a culture that encourages flexible adaptation to change?**

Communication

When an organization plans to undertake an alignment effort, it must communicate throughout the organization how the initiative will affect the organization's processes, methods, and techniques. Leading organizations communicate well, communicate often, and strive to supplement traditional forms of communication such as communication briefings, conferences, seminars, workshops, and meetings with newer online and collaborative methods, such as webcasts. The real measure of whether organizational communication is effective is *not* whether employees feel satisfied with the work they do, but whether their behavior supports strategic objectives.[27]

> **Key question: How does your organization explicitly support communication that encourages the alignment of operations or project work with strategy?**

Commitment

To commit is to pledge yourself to a certain purpose or line of conduct. It means having a sound set of beliefs and, in turn, consistently behaving in accordance with those beliefs. Commitment is persistence with a purpose. We may understand the word *commitment*, but it is grossly underestimated in its ability to make things happen.

In addition to project managers and team members, executive sponsors are also expected to demonstrate a commitment to managing projects. Senior managers must express their ongoing commitment to the process of alignment.[28]

> **Key question: How do your organization's senior managers show their strong commitment to helping project teams?**

Final Thoughts

Some organizations have been successful in aligning strategy and projects, while others need more help. Fortunately, a number of organizational alignment methods are at your disposal. Keep in mind that alignment efforts aren't likely to succeed without involving people, so soft skills are an integral part of the solution.

In summary, here are ten key principles for aligning strategic vision with project work:

- Practice continual and ongoing adjustment based on changes in organizational requirements and external factors.
- Understand the importance of cooperation and take steps to implement it.
- Practice shared leadership and emphasize culture, communication, and commitment.
- Use resource optimization as a guiding factor for alignment.

- Relate metrics to one another at various organizational levels.
- Institute organizational project management processes.
- Follow project portfolio management processes.
- Use information technology for intra-organizational reporting and data management.
- Apply methods to connect business objectives to project objectives.
- Benchmark performance against organizations that successfully practice alignment.

Notes

1 For research emphasizing the importance of aligning strategy and projects and the benefits of alignment, see for example, Project Management Solutions, Inc., *Project Portfolio Management: A Benchmark of Current Business Practices* (Glen Mills, PA: Project Management Solutions, Inc., 2003). Available online at http://www.pmsolutions.com/uploads/file/Research-PPM.pdf (accessed February 3, 2010). For research showing *how* to align strategy and projects, see for example Peter Morris and Ashley Jamieson, *Translating Corporate Strategy into Project Strategy: Realizing Corporate Strategy through Project Management* (Newtown Square, PA: Project Management Institute, 2004).

2 Cathleen Benko and F. Warren McFarlan, *Connecting the Dots: Aligning Projects with Objectives in Unpredictable Times* (Boston: Harvard Business School Press, 2003).

3 Paul C. Dinsmore and Terence J. Cooke-Davies, *Right Projects Done Right: From Business Strategy to Successful Project Implementation* (San Francisco: Jossey-Bass, 2005).

4 Antonio Nieto-Rodriguez and Daniel Evrard, *Boosting Business Performance through Programme and Project Management* (PricewaterhouseCoopers, 2004).

5 Peter Morris and Ashley Jamieson, *Translating Corporate Strategy into Project Strategy: Realizing Corporate Strategy through Project Management* (Newtown Square, PA: Project Management Institute, 2004).

6 Raju Rao, "Connecting Organization Strategy to Projects—The Missing Link," paper presented at the Project Management Institute Global Congress—Asia Pacific, 2007, Hong Kong.

7 Raju Rao, "The Role of Project Management in Transforming a Developing Nation to Developed Status—The Case of India Vision 2020," paper presented at the Project Management Institute Global Congress—Asia Pacific, 2006, Bangkok.

8 Cathleen Benko and F. Warren McFarlan, *Connecting the Dots: Aligning Projects with Objectives in Unpredictable Times* (Boston: Harvard Business School Press, 2003).

9 Project Management Solutions, Inc., *Project Portfolio Management: A Benchmark of Current Business Practices* (Glen Mills, PA: Project Management Solutions, Inc., 2003). Available online at http://www.pmsolutions.com/uploads/file/Research-PPM.pdf (accessed February 3, 2010).

10 Robert Youker and Jerry Brown, "Defining the Hierarchy of Project Objectives," revised paper presented at International Project Management Association World Congress, June 1998, Ljubljana, Slovenia. Available online at http://www.asapm.org/asapmag/articles/m_hierobjs.pdf (accessed February 3, 2010).

11 Wikipedia, "Logical framework approach," http://en.wikipedia.org/wiki/Logical_framework_approach (accessed March 18, 2010).

12 J.H. Sheehan, P.H. Deitz, B.E. Bray, B.A. Harris, and A.B.H. Wong, *The Military Missions and Means Framework*, Interservice/Industry Training, Simulation, and Education Conference (I/ITSEC), 2003.

13 Object Management Group, *Business Motivation Model (BMM) Specifications* (Needham, MA: Object Management Group, 2006).

14 Project Management Association of Japan, *A Guidebook for Project and Program Management for Enterprise Innovation* (Tokyo: Project Management Association of Japan, 2004). Available online at http://www.pmaj.or.jp/ENG/P2M_Download/P2MGuidebookVolume1_060112.pdf (accessed February 3, 2010).

15 Rini van Solingen and Egon Berghout, *The Goal/Question/Metric Method: A Practical Guide* (Columbus, OH: McGraw-Hill, 1999).

16 David Hutchins, *Hoshin Kanri: The Strategic Approach to Continuous Improvement* (Aldershot, UK: Gower Publishing, 2008).

17 Robert Youker and Jerry Brown, "Defining the Hierarchy of Project Objectives," revised paper presented at International Project Management Association World Congress, June 1998, Ljubljana, Slovenia. Available online at http://www.asapm.org/asapmag/articles/m_hierobjs.pdf (accessed February 3, 2010).

18 Ibid.

19 See "Managing the Implementation of Development Projects," World Bank Institute, 2001. See also Robert Youker, "Managing the Implementation of Development Projects," paper presented at Project Management Institute (PMI) Global Congress 2003—North America, Baltimore. Available online at http://www.pm4dev.com/english/

documents/links/Links-2/The_Nature_of_International_Development_ Projects-RY.pdf (accessed January 27, 2010).

20 Project Management Association of Japan, *A Guidebook for Project and Program Management for Enterprise Innovation* (Tokyo: Project Management Association of Japan, 2004). Available online at http://www. pmaj.or.jp/ENG/P2M_Download/P2MGuidebookVolume1_060112.pdf (accessed February 3, 2010).

21 David Hutchins, *Hoshin Kanri: The Strategic Approach to Continuous Improvement* (Aldershot, UK: Gower Publishing, 2008).

22 Peter Morris and Ashley Jamieson, *Translating Corporate Strategy into Project Strategy: Realizing Corporate Strategy through Project Management* (Newtown Square, PA: Project Management Institute, 2004).

23 Ibid., 88.

24 John P. Kotter and James L. Heskett, *Corporate Culture and Performance* (New York: The Free Press, 1992).

25 Jim Highsmith, *Agile Software Development Ecosystems* (Upper Saddle River, NJ: Pearson Education, 2002), 27.

26 Donald T. Tosti and Stephanie Jackson, "Organizational Alignment: How It Works and Why It Matters," *Training Magazine* (April 1994), 58–64.

27 Cees B. M. van Reil and Charles J. Fombrun, *Essentials of Corporate Communications* (New York: Routledge, 2007).

28 For more information on the importance executive commitment has in the success of projects, see *The Standish Group Report: Chaos* (Boston: The Standish Group, 1995), 4. Available online at http://www.projectsmart. co.uk/docs/chaos-report.pdf (accessed February 3, 2010).

CHAPTER 4

Proven Business-Leader Actions for Project Success

Michael O'Brochta, PMP

As a business leader, you are challenged by working in an environment in which your business success is strongly tied to the success of the projects within your business. You are challenged to contribute actively to the success of the projects within your business. But how can you promote project success? This topic has resonated strongly with the thousands of project managers and business leaders whom I have had the pleasure of addressing directly, as well as with the even greater numbers of people who have reacted to articles I have written about this topic in business and project management publications.

The good news for you as a business leader is that you can take proven actions toward project success, and by doing so, you can raise your odds of business success. In this chapter you will:

- Learn why business success is now more dependent on project success
- Find out what proven actions you can take for project success
- Recognize the barriers to your actions
- Learn how to employ familiar management approaches to overcome these barriers.

Why Are Business Leaders Important?

Projects matter. They deliver benefits to customers and to the business. Projects enable a business to accomplish its strategic goals. Projects enable the business leader to succeed. But projects often fail. So businesses fail. So, too, do business leaders.

Who cares? Both senior business leadership and project managers, that's who. One reason the topic of promoting project success seems to get so much traction is the convergence of mutual interests between business leaders, who are working to implement their strategic vision, and project managers, who have an extraordinary focus on delivering results. A June 1999 *Fortune* magazine article reported that the number one reason business leaders fail is "bad execution. As simple as that: not getting things done, being indecisive, not delivering on commitments."[1]

I believe that business leaders who are working to avoid this type of failure have to recognize and embrace their dependency on project management. You as a business leader are in an environment in which work is, with increasing frequency, being conducted as projects and more and more employees are using project management methods. According to the Project Management Institute, the world's leading project-management professional organization, membership and credential holders have doubled in just the past few years to more than 420,000 people worldwide in 70 countries.

The logic seems inescapable to me: You as a business leader are being measured by your ability to deliver business results. Because project management is almost entirely about delivering results, your needs are well served by—even dependent on—project success. Execution matters, to your business and to you.

Just as your success is increasingly dependent on the outcome of projects, project success has become increasingly dependent on you, the business leader. This is where significant opportunities for business-leader action exist—and are desperately needed. According to a survey of federal government program managers conducted by the Office of Management and Budget and the Council for Excellence in Government, more than 80 percent of respondents reported that they receive inadequate support from their business leaders.[2] A broader worldwide survey conducted by Towers Perrin revealed that three-quarters of the employees surveyed "said that their organizations or senior management don't do enough to help them fully engage and contribute to their companies' success."[3]

Project managers have found that project success has become more difficult to achieve in recent years.[4] Projects are more complex, their scope has broadened, and the very definition of success has expanded. In the early days of project management, success was measured predominantly in technical terms. Projects either worked or they didn't. Today, project success has many more dimensions: technical, cost, schedule, customer satisfaction, impact on other projects, and impact on business. The new nature of projects has made project managers more dependent on their business leaders for project success.

Project managers are looking hard for your support as a business leader, and in most places, they are not finding it. They are chomping at the bit for business-leader action. This is a terrific opportunity for the business leader to step forward and take action.

Promoting Project Success

Are you a business leader who:

- Leads an organization that depends on projects and on project managers?

- Is motivated to identify and overcome the barriers to project success?

- Understands the strong relationship between project success and the success of your organization's strategic business objectives, not to mention your own personal success?

- Wants to make a bigger impact on your organization?

If so, there is good news. The business-leader actions for project success are largely known and understood. They have been proven to work. Project management practitioners have been engaged for quite some time in identifying the actions that they would like their business leaders to take for project success. Figure 4-1 lists proven business-leader actions for project success that you can readily adapt. This list has stood the test of time. It was initially developed based on my own experiences in project management—working with thousands of project managers and with business leaders at the Central Intelligence Agency—and also on some excellent writings on this topic that have been published in the past decade.[5]

Choose, Manage, and Organize the Right Projects

The most essential business-leader actions are *organizing work into projects* and *picking the right projects*. Project managers can feel like fish out of water when they work in an environment that does not organize and

- Organize and manage work as projects.
- Pick the right projects.
- Maintain close stakeholder relationships.
- Adhere to a suitable project management process.
- Ensure projects follow a documented plan.
- Ensure projects are based on documented requirements.
- Require a written basis for cost estimates.
- Ensure project resources are commensurate with needs.
- Engage middle management for help.
- Use job performance standards.
- Behave like a servant leader.
- Ask the right questions.

Figure 4-1 Proven Business-Leader Actions

manage work as projects. They may expend a great deal of effort trying to educate stakeholders about and convince them of the merits of basic project components, such as requirements definition, baselines, schedules, and configuration control. This is unproductive and often frustrating for the project manager. It is more efficient if departments or sections are organized in a project-based manner and separated from departments that perform ongoing and repetitive operations.

It is easy for project managers to become overwhelmed if they have too many projects to work on. That's why it is essential to pick the right projects. The project-selection method can be sophisticated (for example, strategic portfolio management) or as simple as choosing only projects the project managers and project teams have the capacity to perform.

The field of organizational project management (OPM), described in greater detail in Chapter 1, is squarely focused on picking the right projects. Organizations are already deriving considerable benefit from OPM approaches, and for those organizations with sufficient maturity to employ OPM, it should be given first consideration. For organizations with limited maturity or limited interest in OPM, I favor the simple approach: Project managers should do only as many projects as can be done well; don't agonize over the decisions about which projects to do.

Formal research about the optimal number of projects a project manager can manage successfully is sparse; however, the few works that I have come across do concur with empirical evidence. Fewer projects are better; fewer projects mean more time spent per project. Fewer projects mean that ultimately, more projects conclude successfully. I think that this is worth emphasizing. If you reduce the overall number of projects, you will likely find that at the end of the year, a greater number of projects have succeeded.

Maintain Close Stakeholder Relationships

Business leaders have a unique responsibility to develop and *maintain close stakeholder and customer relationships* that complement and enhance the relationships formed by the project manager. The time invariably comes when an issue, concern, or decision must be addressed by someone other than the project manager. This type of supportive intervention is often helpful when decisions about project funding, priority, and requirements must be made.

Note that these business-leader relationships should be conducted in such a way that the project manager's authority and responsibility are maintained and the project manager is kept in the loop and well informed. Ideally, the project manager should bring issues to the attention of the business leader.

Adhere to a Suitable Project Management Process

Project management is a discipline, and it is helpful and important to *adhere to a suitable project management process.* Project managers at the top of their game have come to rely on business leaders to *establish a standardized process* for their organization to use. They want to be held accountable for applying tailored versions of this process to each of their projects, and they rely on others to do the same. They can, in the absence of your action, develop and follow their own processes, but they recognize the limits in efficiency and effectiveness of doing so. Wouldn't you rather have project managers managing their projects instead of perpetually reinventing a process each time a new project rolls around?

Ensure Projects Follow a Documented Plan and Are Based on Documented Requirements

Project managers expect business leaders to ensure that they *follow a documented project plan* and that *projects are based on documented requirements.* They expect you to give them adequate time up-front during the initial project phase to build these baseline documents. They should not be pressured to proceed hastily without them. Project managers also expect you to hold them accountable for continuous, controlled revisions to these documents through the project life cycle.

Require a Written Basis for Cost Estimates, and Ensure Project Resources Are Commensurate with Needs

Baseline documents should be backed up with cost estimates that have a *written, definitive basis*. And in return for managing their projects according to plan, project managers should expect their business leaders to ensure that the *project resources* they receive (time, people, and money) are *commensurate with their needs*. If shortages or changes occur, the project manager should not be pressured simply to absorb the effects of the change or do more with less. He or she should give the business leader an impact assessment that explains the effects of the shortage or change. The project manager develops the impact assessment, which could serve as the basis for plan revisions, with regard to the baseline plans, requirements, and other documents.

Engage Middle Management for Help, and Use Job Performance Standards

By *holding middle managers responsible for supporting project managers* and *establishing and using job definitions and performance standards*, ensuring that career progression and growth are aligned with best-practice project management, you will create a long-lasting and sustainable project-based culture.

Behave Like a Servant Leader, and Ask the Right Questions

You can demonstrate your commitment to this positive project-based culture by *asking the right questions* of your project managers. The eight questions listed in Figure 4-2 are a favorite resource of the business leaders with whom I consult. One business leader actually had this list reduced in size and laminated so he could wear it behind his employee badge around his neck and glance casually at it when he found himself in a meeting with project managers. This list helped him to behave like a business leader and ask the right questions.

- What can I do to help?
- What are the requirements?
- What is the plan?
- What is the status compared with the plan?
- What are the top risks and mitigation strategy?
- How do the stakeholders and customers feel?
- What is the basis for your estimates?
- How do you know?

Figure 4-2 Questions Business Leaders Should Ask

This list will help you minimize the traditional distractions: getting too involved in the project details, trying to solve the project issues, or doing the project managers' jobs for them. Like my list of business-leader actions, I have developed this list over time. At this point, I consider it to be stable, though I do occasionally add or subtract from it.

At the top of the list is an extraordinarily effective question: "What can I do to help?" This supportive and effective approach to management has become more popular since the term *servant leadership* came into use to describe the executive's role.[6] Servant leadership continues to be regarded by the *Harvard Business Review* and other sources as the basis for the modern management theory that leaders should be led by the group's needs. Your role as a business leader is enhanced when you behave like a servant leader by supporting project managers. In such a culture, you will attract, retain, and grow project management excellence.

Tailoring Business-Leader Actions

You can, and in fact should, readily adapt my list of business-leader actions to suit your specific needs in your own organization. And given the intense interest project managers have in this topic, who better to turn to for help when adapting this list than project managers themselves? I recommend that you reach out to a few selected project managers and ask them to customize the list.

Choosing someone to do this is an important decision. Ideally, you will identify a few project managers who have demonstrated an interest in and an aptitude for maturing not only the efforts within the scope of their projects, but also the organization's initiatives. I recommend picking individuals who understand and are skilled at managing projects, who have encountered limitations in achieving project success, who already recognize their dependence on the business leader to overcome these limitations, and who understand your genuine interest in faithfully carrying out some of the actions on the list.

Busting Business-Leader Barriers

It is essential to acknowledge that you probably *cannot* accomplish all the actions on the list. Even those business leaders predisposed to action will find that their circumstances and the pressures of their jobs make it difficult at best to actively work toward project success. Some factors that will challenge business-leader action include:

- Work volume
- Organizational maturity level
- Change-readiness level
- Limited authority.

Work Volume and Organizational Maturity Level

The volume of work—important work—that is already within the business leader's domain is significant. Time and resources for carrying out these actions for project success may be very limited. Additionally, your organization will itself impose limitations on what can be done. Your organization's level of maturity limits what it is capable of accomplishing even if the necessary time and resources are available. If your organization's projects are characterized by last-minute heroics, ad hoc activity, and a lack of formal processes, you should choose only an item or two from the list of business-leader actions. By contrast, business leaders who work in organizations with well-defined, repeatable processes that undergo continuous improvement have the latitude to undertake a greater number of items on the list.

The actions on the list are strategic and long-term. If you are able to pick only a limited number of them to enact today, you will have another opportunity tomorrow to chip away at more of them. Patience is, after all, a virtue.

Change-Readiness Level

Likewise, your organization's change-readiness level will affect the timing of your action. Some organizations are more change-ready than others. It does little good for you to push for a change if individuals or the organization is not ready. In fact, this is counterproductive and sours the well water for future attempts at similar changes.

Organizations with high-readiness levels are characterized by strong desires for change and readiness for it. A strong resistance to change indicates a low readiness level. Moderate-readiness levels are characterized by a desire for change but a lack of readiness. For example, if there were a merger yesterday, and if today there was a reorganization, then tomorrow would not be a good time for you to try to implement a substantial change to something as significant as the standard corporate product development life cycle process. A more appropriate business-leader action would be to grant approval for a single project that would alter the standard life cycle in a way that benefits the project but does not broadly impact other projects and processes in the organization.

Your actions as a business leader must conform to the change-readiness level of the organization. By waiting until the time is right, you will accomplish more than if you rush to take actions for which the organization is not ready.

Limited Authority

Appearing near the top of the list of barriers for many business leaders are politics and limitations in authority. There will be limits on what you can do in any organization. No surprise. Business leaders I have worked with have reported that both politics and limitations on authority represent leading sources of conflicting demands, serve as the source of scope creep and shifting focus of projects in their domain, and are responsible for fluctuations in priority and resource availability.

The good news here is that you can amplify your authority to overcome many political and other limitations. Techniques to amplify your authority include:

- Practicing servant leadership
- Communicating effectively
- Assuming a level of authority
- Forming a project management council.

When adapted, these familiar techniques can serve your needs in a project-based environment.

Practicing Servant Leadership

One powerful approach for amplifying your authority is to practice servant leadership. We have already seen that this approach is the cornerstone for behaving like a business leader and asking the right questions. Remarkably, it also forms the foundation for amplifying authority. This authority, referred to as *power* by some authors, can come from a number of sources.[7] Although some of the sources of power are limited by circumstances that you can do little about, other sources can be amplified through the practice of servant leadership. You can build strong bonds and loyalty with others simply by taking interest in their professional well-being. Helping people will result in their vesting additional power in you. You can and should use this power/authority to overcome some of the barriers to taking proven actions for project success.

Communicating Effectively

Similarly, you can amplify your authority through effective communication. Although you, as well as practically every other forward-thinking business leader, probably already understand the importance of communicating effectively, the real challenge is doing it.

I am compelled by the results of a study of more than 5,000 project managers and their stakeholders, including business leaders, that addressed the differences between what we know we should do and what we actually do. The study examined how the top two percent, the strongest performers, the "Alphas," differed from everyone else.[8] While virtually all of the study participants knew that effective communication was important, the Alphas communicated twice as effectively and did so twice as often as the non-Alphas. Both groups worked under similar constraints; both had precious little extra time for added effort. Yet, somehow, the Alphas managed to communicate twice as much and twice as effectively. Remarkable.

Assuming a Level of Authority

Interestingly, similar results in the Alpha study were observed regarding authority in general. Alphas acted as if they already had the necessary authority. They acted as if they had twice as much authority as the non-Alphas, when in fact, both groups had the same levels of authority. Again, remarkable.

Forming a Project Management Council

And now for the "silver bullet" approach to amplifying authority: forming a project management council. This is a favorite approach of mine.

Project management councils (also called project support offices, project management working groups, project management offices, strategic project offices, project management centers of excellence, and project management communities of practice) are organizations formed explicitly for the purpose of focusing on how project management is, can be or should be practiced within an organization.

A project management council can be key to amplifying your authority and to acting on that authority. It can help you develop a tailored list of proven business-leader actions for project success, and it can be a resource you draw upon when carrying out those actions. (Because these actions will transform your business, you should see that they are managed as a business transformation project; see Chapter 6 for an in-depth discussion of transformation.)

I have seen project management councils work well in virtually all situations: for business leaders with limited time, in organizations with differing maturity levels or change-readiness levels, and in various political environments. Many others also have had success with project management councils during the past decade.[9]

My ideal project management council is composed entirely of motivated project managers who have volunteered for the assignment. They are experienced, visionary change agents. As thought leaders, they know how project management is done and how it should be done. They care deeply about their chosen profession and are concerned with the well-being of other project managers.

I view a project management council as a link between the business leader and project managers and vice versa. To help it gain recognition for its good work and to counter many of the negative stereotypes associated with groups of this type (those that exist outside the formal organization chart), it should comprise no more than about a dozen people, it should be chaired or sanctioned by a business leader, and it should have limited authority. It also should focus broadly on the entire organizational system relative to projects and project management. Endow the council with enduring value by tasking it with making recommendations to business leaders and helping implement the proven business-leader actions for project success. Minimize the possibility that it will be viewed as a threat to established organizational decision-making mechanisms by preventing it from having control over decisions and resources. Limiting members' terms to a year or possibly two will ensure a constant flow of fresh perspectives and ideas.

Final Thoughts

I have presented what I think is a good-news story to you, the business leader: You can promote project success by taking action. Together we have examined the critical dependency between business-leader success and project success. I have:

- Listed proven business-leader actions for project success and encouraged you to adapt the list by seeking the advice of project managers in your organization
- Acknowledged the barriers that may make it challenging for business leaders to implement these actions
- Discussed familiar approaches the business leader can employ to break down these barriers
- Described approaches that will amplify your power to take action, with an emphasis on servant leadership
- Strongly encouraged you to form a project management council, which will help you develop a customized action list and implement the actions.

By working together, business leaders and project managers will likely find both organizational and project success.

Notes

1 Ram Charan, "Why CEOs Fail," *Fortune*, June 21, 1999.
2 Council for Excellence in Government, "Delivering Program Results," *The Public Manager* 37, no. 4, December 2008, 6.
3 *Towers Perrin Global Workforce Study*, October 22, 2007. Available online at http://www.towersperrin.com/tp/showhtml.jsp?url=global/publications/gws/index.htm&country=global (accessed February 1, 2010), 2.
4 Marcia Jedd, "In Command," PM Network, February 2006, reviewed paper by Michael O'Brochta, "Getting Executives to Act for Project Success," 58.
5 See for example Robert J. Graham and Randall L. Englund, *Creating an Environment for Successful Projects, Second Edition* (San Francisco: Jossey-Bass, 2003), and Tomas Blomquist and Ralf Muller, *Middle Managers in Program & Project Portfolio Management: Practices, Roles & Responsibilities* (Newtown Square, PA: Project Management Institute, 2006).
6 Robert K. Greenleaf's 1977 book *Servant Leadership: A Journey into the Nature of Legitimate Power and Greatness* (New York: Paulist Press) has been followed by many other publications on the topic, including Michael Useem's article, "The Leadership Lessons of Mount Everest," published in the *Harvard Business Review on Breakthrough Leadership* (Boston: Harvard Business School Publishing, 2002), 151.
7 In a now-classic 1959 study, "The Bases of Social Power," social psychologists John French and Bertram Raven developed a schema of five categories of power: positional, referent, expert, reward, and coercive.
8 Andy Crowe, *Alpha Project Managers: What the Top 2% Know That Everyone Else Does Not* (Atlanta, GA: Velociteach, 2006).
9 Brian Hobbs addresses the status of project management councils and similarly named groups in his 2007 white paper for the Project Management Institute, "The Multi-Project PMO: A Global Analysis of the Current State of Practice."

CHAPTER 5

Executive Imperatives: The Role of Project Sponsorship in Organizational Success

Randall Englund

Are you responsible for sponsoring projects? What guidelines and philosophies influence your thoughts, actions, and conversations? How do you inspire and lead motivated people to discover and implement effective project practices? How do sponsors in your organization ensure that all projects deliver outcomes that support corporate strategies? What corporate plans or project sponsorship initiatives are in place in your organization to optimize business outcomes?

These are key issues for corporate leaders and senior project management professionals who sponsor or work on complex projects, so in this chapter, we explore the essential components of a successful project sponsorship program. You will learn:

- About key project sponsorship imperatives—efforts that are necessary, commanding, take priority, and must be done
- How sponsors create an environment that promotes greater achievement through project work—one in which effective projects and efficient processes produce desired results

- Critical success factors for sponsors and how they link to organizational success.

This chapter offers guidance based on experience and case studies that will help executives improve their performance and achieve greater results from project-based work. This chapter may also help project managers learn to *manage up* the organization, which means taking the initiative to understand the larger business environment, then questioning, mentoring, coaching, and guiding their managers to do the right things.

Excellence in Project Work

Organizations want to optimize business outcomes—revenue, effectiveness, or cost reduction. A key executive imperative is a focus on creating excellence *in* projects, programs, and portfolios. Creating excellence in project management is the application of methodologies, viewpoints, insights, and leading practices to get results from project-based work. Focusing attention on these efforts can facilitate the refinement of an organization's operating processes.

Green Leadership

The progressive improvement of practices, which is also called *organizational maturity*, requires that project leaders and management reduce organizational "toxins" and create "green" organizations. In this context, *green* means that the physical, tangible efforts to improve the environment are extended into the nonphysical, intangible personal working relationships that affect our working environments. Green is good. A productive, desirable green environment is characterized by:

- Trust among colleagues and management
- Cooperation instead of competition

- A common sense of purpose that provides sustenance and meaning to all activities
- A shared vision that brings clarity to the direction of work
- Frequent, open communication
- An atmosphere in which individuals are respected, able to express their creativity, and have the power to influence others through positive persuasive techniques.

A green project sponsor engages people in open discussions, even if dissent is present, to determine the best way to proceed on a complex project. Cultivating a green environment is necessary if all stakeholders are to buy into, create, and support complex project work.

Without a green foundation, organizations experience failures and overruns, and stakeholders are dissatisfied. These "toxic" project environments are usually created by political practices that make everyone uneasy and frustrated—except those who have the power to benefit from them. Managers who barely understand or appreciate the project management process also contribute to a negative environment, as do sponsors who:

- Fail to communicate
- Mistrust staff or team members
- Require burdensome reporting or the use of misguided metrics.

Every sponsor and project manager has the power within himself or herself to embrace a change in thinking and act upon it every day. But while implementing a green environment is laudable and necessary, it is not sufficient to create a truly excellent organization. What is also required is an overt, explicit effort to achieve successful outcomes through project management.

Excellence through Project Work

After working to create a green environment, the next sponsor imperative is to focus on creating excellence *through* projects, programs, and portfolios.

Creating excellence through project management means achieving greater results from project-based work, which helps an organization realize competitive advantage by executing strategy through projects in a portfolio and making significant advancements in the maturity of people, processes, and the environment of a project-based organization.

Aligning Projects and Strategies

Progress comes in steps. An organization works to improve its project, program, and portfolio management processes. At some point, these disciplines are optimized, and everybody easily sees how they contribute to positive business outcomes. What are the signs that an organization has optimized its project, program, and portfolio management processes?

- Less attention can be focused on the "means" because those processes function smoothly and are easily adapted or updated when necessary.

- More attention can be given to the "ends"—the reasons the organization exists. Executives can focus on strategic execution, from the organization's purpose and identity to operational performance.

The imperative facing executives in all organizations is not only to embark on a quest to improve management processes, but also to create a green environment that facilitates project-based work that achieves desired outcomes. This quest and role are best assumed by project sponsors on projects they directly sponsor and by executives who sponsor programs and portfolios. These sponsors need to eliminate "pollutants" and toxic actions that demoralize project managers and their teams. This means searching with unrelenting curiosity for best practices—wander around the project space, interview stakeholders, conduct open-ended surveys, go to conferences, read books and trade journals, solicit expert opinions, and look for ideas in other industries or disciplines. People closest to the work often have excellent ideas about how to improve—take the time to ask them about their experiences. When you discover best practices, be prepared to take action. Pursuing best practices allows you to move from

- Cloudy to clear outcomes
- Hazy to heroic actions
- Toxic to green outcomes.

The success or failure of any project often hinges on how well the project sponsor—the person who funds the project, supports it throughout, and ensures that desired benefits are achieved—relates to the project, the project manager, and other stakeholders. However, executives who are assigned as project sponsors often have little if any experience understanding their roles and responsibilities during the project life cycle. What happens when a sponsor lacks experience in the role?

Here are some responses to a recent survey on project sponsorship issues conducted in a variety of organizations:

- "If the project sponsor doesn't understand what is being managed, then they may fail when they attempt to micromanage the project."
- "There is a lot of variability in our organization depending on which projects and which departments are involved. Some are better than others."
- "Sponsors here at our company seem to only be good at signing checks, rather than having an understanding of what is needed."
- "Most often, it appears sponsors are 'overcome by events' and lose sight of the accumulation of minor impacts along the way."
- "People play the role of sponsor by default because of their position but do not actively participate as sponsors in our department."
- "Some areas are better than other areas within our company. In general, I believe those that are not as good lack the awareness of what is expected."
- "Most of the sponsors hand you a project, and that is the last you see of them until there is a problem."

Would project participants in your organization make similar statements? How prepared are you to be a project sponsor?

Critical Sponsor Success Factors

Success starts with a strong commitment to improve. Leaders become better prepared to be sponsors of major projects by taking inventory of their talents, skills, and behaviors and putting appropriate action plans in place. Ask each sponsor on each project to take the quiz in Figure 5-1. Think of it as a checklist that will help sponsors move toward excellence. The quiz can provide insight into sponsors' strengths or limitations, as well as environmental obstacles that might limit project success.

Developing Effective Sponsor/Project Relationships

Problems in communication and execution are inevitable as long as upper managers and project managers do not understand the mechanics of their relationship. Upper managers often insist on doing things their way, even if they are new to that position or portion of the business and do not understand project management. For example, upper management was once pushing me to become a technical expert on a project I was managing. They insisted that this knowledge was necessary to earn respect. I argued that a project manager's responsibility is to drive the overall process and get issues resolved, not to try to second-guess the technical experts. The executives and I did not resolve our disagreements in the initial conversation but agreed to keep each other informed as the project progressed.

During this project, upper management criticized me for a change my project team made. The team had discussed the change thoroughly. It took courage and passion on my part to push back against the manager, who was basing his reaction on input from others, not his own experience or knowledge. I had the strength of the whole team, the soundness of our

Check the column that best describes your typical response	Often	Sometimes	Not often
• The sponsor's goals for the project are clear.			
• The sponsor believes there is a real need for the project.			
• The sponsor understands how many people or groups will be affected by the project.			
• The sponsor knows what resources are needed for the project to be successful.			
• The sponsor is willing to commit the resources needed for the project to succeed.			
• The sponsor publicly conveys the organization's strong commitment to the project and its desired outcomes.			
• The sponsor uses appropriate rewards and pressures to gain support for the project.			
• The sponsor ensures that procedures to track progress and problems are established.			
• The sponsor is aware of all commitments that are required for the project to succeed.			
• The sponsor shows consistent, sustained support for the project.			

Figure 5-1 Project Sponsor Competencies

Adapted with permission from Randall Englund and Alfonso Bucero, *Project Sponsorship: Achieving Management Commitment for Project Success* (San Francisco: Jossey-Bass, 2006), 116–120.

deliberations, and my own belief that this was the right thing to do working in my favor. The manager backed down.

Throughout this project I consistently applied sound project management practices and achieved success. How did I do it?

- I earned respect by being consistent in my actions.
- I got difficult projects done and in ways that went beyond upper management's own knowledge.
- I kept the manager informed of what I was doing so he would not be surprised.
- I also made sure, through regular communication, that I had his support for the general direction of the project.

This approach helped me avoid being micromanaged by the manager, because he respected my contributions. He and his manager, who had limited familiarity with project management, came to recognize that the project manager makes a unique, valuable contribution. They witnessed how masterfully the discipline can be applied.

The executive imperative is to recognize these talented individuals in your organization—and get out of their way.

Developing a Clear Scope

As a project manager, I often have to run projects I had little involvement in selecting and little involvement in deciding what they should accomplish. For instance, I was once given the charter to get a team together and quickly fix all prototype defects for a new technical product where rapid time to market was a priority. However, most of the functional managers did not want other people working on modules for which they were responsible. The real problem that surfaced during my discussions with key stakeholders was that when a defect in a module was reported but the cause was not immediately obvious, people wasted valuable time by pointing a finger at others, assigning blame, or brushing the problem aside. ("It's not my job.")

I repurposed the high-powered cross-functional team to focus only on quickly identifying problem sources; the responsible functional areas remained responsible for fixes. This solution worked wonderfully because everyone wanted to eliminate unproductive tasks or conversations that wasted time, and they appreciated help in focusing on what caused the defects. The modified process that I developed to solve the problems came into being because I, as the project manager, pushed back against the chartered assignment and insisted on clarifying what the project needed to accomplish.

Situations like this are common. Sometimes the outcome of a proposed project is unclear, or the project appears to be the wrong solution to a stakeholder's or customer's needs—which amounts to working on a solution in search of a problem. Whenever a project team accepts an assignment without a clear problem statement that everyone agrees upon, it is set up to fail. Project team members need courage, time, and willingness to push back. What can project stakeholders do when faced with problems like these? Consistently apply sound project management practices:

- Get involved earlier in project initiations.
- Take the time to interview key stakeholders and as many senior managers as possible, and clarify project goals with the sponsor. Making this extra effort surfaces *real* problems that need to be solved and helps you determine the true definition of success for the project so that you can meet stakeholders' requirements.

The executive imperative is to establish a portfolio management process that links execution to strategic goals, defines criteria for project selection, prioritizes projects and programs, and communicates this information to all project stakeholders. Furthermore, sponsors need to expect project managers and other stakeholders to push back against ambiguous assignments. Both sides need to engage in negotiations about the objectives and constraints for each project; clearly define problems; prioritize the importance of solutions and the approach to those problems; and set expectations.

Creating a Positive Sponsorship Culture

Successful executives are open to coaching from below. They not only welcome these inputs but actively seek them. In our research on project sponsorship, we found a number of examples of how project managers can manage upward. Project managers can influence upper management by:

- "Selling" the role of project sponsor to upper managers by emphasizing the value of sponsorship and the benefits that accrue to the organization when it is done well:
  - An improved standing and profile within the organization; important projects may propel project sponsors to success. (Although it's also important to keep in mind that failed projects may hinder their professional success).
  - Being linked with an exciting and very successful project; exciting projects have high visibility in organizations.
  - An opportunity for the project sponsor to promote his or her professional background and prestige.
  - Public exposure, including official launches, presentation evenings, and mentions in media.
  - Getting an agenda implemented. Sponsorship represents an opportunity to turn a vision into reality using assigned resources.
- Asking their sponsors what they do and do not know about the projects the sponsors are involved in. This question is not meant to expose ignorance but to get their attention.
- Creating a training program on project sponsorship.

- Getting executive commitment to engage fully in the sponsorship role.
- Establishing agreement about next steps (an action plan).

The ideal situation is proactive sponsorship—having a project sponsor who is committed, accountable, serious about the project, knowledgeable, trained, and able not only to talk the talk but also to walk the walk. Such people are trustworthy in all respects. Their values are transparent and aligned with the organization and its strategy. Such sponsors protect project teams from disruptive outside influences and back them up when times are tough. Sponsors set the tone for how people operate in their organizations.

The best way to sustain good sponsorship is to start out with good sponsorship. It is far better to start out with the right sponsor than to have to repair a bad sponsorship situation later. That is why it is so important to select the right sponsor in the first place and to train the person for the role. An organization's goal should be to develop a mature organizational culture that is committed to this approach.

A lack of good project sponsorship is a major cause of problems on projects. Conversely, well-executed sponsorship by senior executives brings better project results. Creating a defined sponsor selection process and a development path, providing ongoing mentoring and constructive evaluation and feedback, and applying knowledge management all contribute to a culture in which good sponsorship can grow.

The executive imperative is to get educated about the role of project sponsorship and to set specific organizational goals about what it means to achieve excellence in project sponsorship. These might include sending all sponsors to a training course, ensuring that all projects have individual sponsors assigned and active throughout the project, and having sponsors present a summary of benefits achieved through projects and programs at a quarterly review.

Developing an Improved Set of Project Philosophies

Executives need training, experience, and practice to be effective sponsors. Sponsorship is a required and critical success factor for all projects in all industries and disciplines. Every organization needs to keep moving forward. Every day is a good day for change. With that in mind, what are some imperatives that might need to change in your environment? Things to consider, for example, could include embracing failure; providing more feedback; or the differences between controlling people and managing to outcomes.

Embracing Failure

I believe sponsors need to rethink their views about failure. The only real failure is failing to learn from each and every project, regardless of the outcome.

I once conducted a pilot of a new training program to determine if the program was ready to go. It was not, but I considered the pilot project successful because I found all the problems and was ready to address them. The design team, however, was devastated that it could not go back to the company celebrating the launch of the new program. This attitude inhibited team members' ability to look closely at what worked and what did not. I was ready to suggest a number of improvements, but they were not ready to listen. The project sponsor was present but did nothing to intervene. I later spoke to the head of the company about this prevailing attitude of "get it right the first time out." He was aware of it and concerned about it, and he said he would like to change it. But he never did, and neither the program nor the company exists in the same form today.

A green environment facilitates consistent, predictable, and sustainable success, in part because every project is viewed as a means to improve. The focus is on overall organizational success, not just on individual project performance. People then feel as if they are constantly contributing to organizational and personal knowledge. The point is to "get it right the last time"—meaning that experimentation, trial and error, bad ideas, foolishness, fun times, craziness, scrappiness, collaboration, and creativity all have their place, and together, they finally lead to a successful outcome.

Kimberly Wiefling of Wiefling Consulting said of failure:

I do a lot of work in Japan, where failure is 'fatal' … or at least it was in the past. Now there is a new understanding of failure sweeping Japan, the notion of 'failing forward.' How do I know? I started it! Although quite a few people with whom I have worked feared failure enough to avoid setting goals entirely, my Japanese colleagues seem to particularly need to reinvent their relationship with failure. The concept of failing forward, of failure as a foundation of success, brings increased willingness to take on more risk, innovate, and create. If we aren't allowed to fail we can't start anything! I say build a tall junk pile and learn from it.[1]

Sandra Clark of the University of California Santa Cruz Extension added:

At a brainstorming meeting I sometimes will ask for bad/wrong answers and throw out candy to everyone who comes up with a 'bad' idea. I like the idea of rewarding the bravery needed in taking risks. Everyone seems so paranoid to say something wrong that we edit out a lot of great ideas before we even begin. I'm thinking of having buttons made that say 'I took a risk and failed.'[2]

The executive imperative is to support organizational learning, even at the risk of tolerating some failures. Sponsors at all levels set the tone for how failure and learning are perceived. Take the time to share thinking, standards, and expectations. Provide appropriate rewards not only for successes but also for failures that led to heightened understanding about risks, things to avoid, and innovative approaches. The goal is to set a higher priority for continuous learning that is then recycled into new best practices.

Providing More Feedback

A course I took during my graduate studies required us to submit a case study every week. The instructor graded the submitted cases but made no comments, and no discussion about the cases occurred in the classroom. Over the duration of the course, there was little noticeable improvement in the quality of the cases the students submitted or the grades we received. In another course, the instructor read aloud sample comments from each case after we submitted the first one and made numerous comments on the cases handed back to the students each week. Both the quality of submittals and the grades we received improved markedly during the course.

This lesson made an indelible impression on me about the power of feedback. Every manager has this tool in his or her kit, but he or she needs to decide to use it. Project management maturation happens when people get feedback on what they do well as well as suggestions on how to do things better. This kind of feedback is so powerful that it can minimize the need to point out what people are doing wrong. When strengths are praised and reinforced, weaknesses fall by the wayside. Unfortunately, many people feel compelled to point out others' failings, even though positive feedback is what actually boosts people's potential to achieve.

High-performing project teams, which are so important for achieving excellence in organizations, are ones in which members regularly submit their work to each other to improve their work and achieve their goals. They are less competitive and more collaborative. No one is expected to get the work right the first time or on his or her own. Peer reviews, driven by a shared value of accountability for the success of the team, project, and organization, produce excellent results. (We used extensive peer reviews at the HP Project Management Initiative, a corporate project office whose purpose was to lead the continuous improvement of project management across the company.[3])

Given that most professionals have some discretionary control over what they work on or where they spend their time, and that they probably have multiple projects to work on, how can sponsors get stakeholders to give top priority to their projects? This question has multiple answers, and most people are well served by asking the question every day throughout their careers. The answer is probably different for each individual you work with. While there is no one right answer, a best practice is for the sponsor to simply provide as much feedback as possible. In an environment in which feedback is scarce, people who regularly and promptly provide constructive responses stand out. Stakeholders may prioritize work on which they know they will get useful feedback.

Early feedback that corrects how a repetitive process is used is always welcome because it saves on rework. Suggestions on revising the order in which material is presented are wonderful—they allow for easy corrections that immensely improve value. A person who takes the time to provide this feedback may be treasured as a rare commodity. Other types of valuable feedback include making comments on a report or paper, asking questions that prompt additional research, acknowledging material that works well or evokes interest and could be expanded, pointing out parts of written work that are unclear, and showing enthusiastic support for a course of action.

Hardly anyone appreciates a leader whose "lights are on, but nobody is home." Leaders need to make it a high priority to respond to every inquiry; share their thinking processes; develop and use consistent criteria when making decisions; communicate all news, good or bad; provide reflective answers to questions; temper both their own and team members' anxiety; encourage others to speak up; and generally become known for giving quality responses. They need to understand the ebb and flow of team dynamics, using their discretion to decide when to push and when to let natural energy drive the process. These behaviors demonstrate that the leader is paying attention to all the people who are responsible for the success of the project, program, or portfolio.

The executive imperative and case for giving feedback hinges on establishing shared values and putting them into practice. The results will be extraordinary. Craft a clear, concise, convincing, and compelling vision statement about portfolio success. Help all project and program stake-holders visualize how their roles contribute to that success. Early in each project, take the time to emphasize the importance of each person's contribution. Make explicit commitments to be accountable for overall success and to extract the optimum contribution from each other. Work to demonstrate these values every day, both by soliciting feedback from and providing it to others. Regularly recognize results that project and program teams contribute to organizational success.

Controlling People versus Managing to Outcomes

Project work leaves us floating in an ocean of data and disconnected facts that overwhelm us with choices. The core choice on projects is between control and results. If control is more important, the cost is weaker results. If results are more important, the cost is giving up some control. Getting more of one requires sacrificing a portion of the other. Onerous controls inhibit achievement of intended results because they demoralize people and limit how they approach creative work.

It may be necessary to give up a sense of control to get results. Control, after all, is an illusion. Nature is firmly rooted in chaos. People try to con-vince themselves, and their bosses, that they are in control of their projects. They may come close to achieving this illusion of control, and project managers, through their close access to task owners, progress reports, and performance metrics, are usually far more knowledgeable about the project or program than anyone else. Try as they may, however, the fact remains that far more forces are at work in our universe than people can ever understand or control. This, however, does not relieve executives or their staff of the obligation to achieve results. What should you do?

It takes courage to make tough calls. Resolve conflicting values and dilemmas by engaging in dialogue with key stakeholders. Trust your judg-ment about what is most important. Take a stand on which value you choose at the point of paradox—the point at which it becomes impossible to achieve both values. What is most important: Being a hero or a planner? Control or results? Output or outcome? You can then pursue both values up to the point at which the two actually conflict; at that point, you must choose, and make clear to others, what is most important.

Changing the direction of an organization to achieve new outcomes, such as adopting new technologies or entering new markets, is a big challenge that may benefit from a concerted effort to manage change. A wise move is to charter a project office to lead this change effort, not by brute force or command and control, but by following a proven change management process. Executives need to work hand in hand to provide the leadership, learning, earning, means, and motivation to guide this process.[4]

The executive imperative is to focus on results and constantly correct the course to stay on track. Capture the minimum of data required to stay informed. Seek information that supports action-oriented decision-making. Just because you can capture every conceivable piece of information does not mean you should, nor can most organizations afford to do so. Producing excessive reports and running lots of metrics in an attempt to "feel comfortable" is not advisable. To relieve anxiety, continuously dialogue with stakeholders and reinforce intended results.

A Challenge to Sponsors

At the PMI Northern California Symposium 2008 at Stanford University, Esteri Hinman, a capability owner at Intel's corporate platform office, included in her presentation a challenge, written in the form of a letter to executives:

Dear Executive,

We know you want to change the way we do business *now*. We recognize the business needs driving that change. But it isn't that simple. Transformational change takes time, lots of time. Our own people will struggle against that change. Changing people is hard work. Here's how you can help us....

- Don't give out a mandate unless you have the fortitude to stay with it through the years.
- Provide clear prioritization. We can't change everything at the same time.
- Celebrate the baby steps—loudly.
- Above all, remember this is about changing people's *behavior*. Model the behaviors we want, and *catch people doing it right*.

Sincerely,

Your Corporate Change Agents

P.S. If you can't do these things for us, please destroy this letter, and ignore the team behind the curtain.[5]

Hinman has found through experience that if you cannot get whole-hearted, 100 percent support (which is very rare) from executives, it is more effective in the long run for project managers to fly under the radar.[6] The executive imperative is to create an environment of support.

My experiences make it clear to me that much more executive support is needed in today's organizations if they truly wish not only to survive but to prosper by creating value through project-based work.

Believe that positive results are possible but may not follow a clearly defined path. A sponsor imperative is to focus on creating excellence in projects, programs, and portfolios, which is accomplished by focusing on people, processes, and the working environment. Put checks in place to ensure that all initiatives are green, not toxic, with regard to human dynamics. Believe that these efforts will reap the results that the organization is chartered to produce. Recognize the value created through projects and programs within a portfolio, and make it a priority to support everything that enables that value-creation process. Set a goal to create excellence in project sponsorship. Be flexible and enjoy the ride!

Critical Success Factors

- Recognize the huge impact that effective project sponsorship has on project successes and the accompanying responsibilities.
- Clarify project sponsors' roles and responsibilities, and implement a training program to instill these values within each person assigned to sponsor projects.
- Consciously create green working environments that encourage excellence from project team members.
- Actively participate in defining desired outcomes and setting expectations for all project work; be present to guide teams through variances that may be either detrimental or necessary for project success.
- Lead with authenticity and integrity; set an example for others to follow.

Notes

1   Kimberly Wiefling, in response to "Embracing Failure," a blog entry by Randall Englund, posted at the UCSC Extension in Silicon Valley website on January 4, 2007. Online at http://svprojectmanagement.com/embracing-failure (accessed February 19, 2010).
2   Sandra Clark, in response to "Embracing Failure," a blog entry by Randall Englund, posted at the UCSC Extension in Silicon Valley website on January 4, 2007. Online at http://svprojectmanagement.com/embracing-failure (accessed February 19, 2010).
3   See Robert J. Graham and Randall L. Englund, *Creating an Environment for Successful Projects*, 2nd ed. (San Francisco: Jossey-Bass, 2004), Chapter 9.
4   See Randall Englund, Robert Graham, and Paul Dinsmore, *Creating the Project Office: A Manager's Guide to Leading Organizational Change* (San Francisco: Jossey-Bass, 2003).

5 See "A Letter to Executives," a blog entry by Randall Englund, posted at the UCSC Extension in Silicon Valley website on September 24, 2008, and the corresponding response from Esteri Hinman. Online at http://svprojectmanagement.com/a-letter-to-executives (accessed February 19, 2010).
6 Ibid.

CHAPTER 6

Successful Business Transformation

Folake Dosunmu, PMP, PgMP, OPM3

Are your corporate objectives threatened by the significant forces of competitive and chaotic environmental change? What corporate plans or initiatives are in place in your organization to take advantage of new opportunities or implement new initiatives? Are the multiple work streams needed to manage these projects effectively organized to articulate and respond to the challenges of change?

These are key questions for corporate leaders and senior project management professionals who are initiating or working on transformation projects. In this chapter, we will explore several essential components of a successful business transformation, including:

- The definition of *business transformation*
- Trends driving transformation
- The prevalent types of transformation
- Examples of transformational organizations
- The benefits of business transformation
- The role of executive leadership in business transformation
- Barriers to success and what can be done to overcome them.

Critical Business Conditions

In April 2008, U.S. Federal Reserve chairman Ben Bernanke informed Congress that a recession in the United States was a possibility. The recession, of course, happened, and it is one of a growing number of challenges that CEOs face. These include an inability to predictably generate growth, the fast pace needed to sustain customer interest, managing innovation, and maintaining customer loyalty. Many businesses have been forced to change focus and direction to stay competitive. Business leaders realize that to achieve and maintain growth, organizations must turn to innovative approaches that deliver dramatic changes and initiate business transformation. Business success is ultimately about the business: what it is, how it is run, and how it satisfies customer needs through its product.

In April 2009, the Federal Reserve Board continued to express, in very guarded language, their continuing concern about economic weakness. What will the story be in April 2012? Will the U.S. unemployment rate continue to climb to new highs? Will the business implications of the dollar's weakness be fully understood? Will the cumulative impact of U.S. government deficits and financial weakness cause inflation or deflation? We don't fully know. What we do know is that these factors are transforming the world in unpredictable ways.

Business Survival

Every morning in Africa, a gazelle wakes up. It knows it must run faster than the fastest lion or it will be killed. Every morning a lion wakes up. It knows it must outrun the slowest gazelle or it will starve to death. It doesn't matter if you are a lion or a gazelle. When the sun comes up, you'd better be running.[1]

Businesses, too, must outrun the competition if they want to survive. Even the smallest companies can become lions. With no prior experience in the call-center industry, Rick Diamond, former CEO of call-center company ACI Telecentrics, and his partner Gary Cohen recognized that they had to do at least one thing better than their competition, or their company would starve. So every morning they asked themselves, "How can we catch the competition, and how can we improve upon what they do?" The answers to these questions led to a business transformation project. One of the benefits of this transformation project was the creation of the technology for predictive dialing, which soon became the industry standard and helped ACI grow from two employees to 2,200.[2]

If you are chasing the competition, be a lion. Ask yourself, "How can we catch the competition? How can we improve upon what they do?" If you are trying to stay ahead of the competition, run like a gazelle. Ask yourself, "How can we avoid being caught? What will allow us to increase the distance between ourselves and the competition?"[3] To survive this economy and flourish in the future, businesses today must outrun the competition when the sun comes up, or they will starve to death—no matter the nature of the business.

Business Transformation

Before we delve more deeply into transformation, it is important to provide a working definition of business transformation, sometimes called *business change management, corporate renewal,* or *business improvement.* For the purposes of this chapter, the term *business transformation* is used to refer to a C-level leadership initiative geared toward corporate renewal that comprises an array of competitive, strategic, enterprise-wide change projects that have a profound impact on the organization's capabilities, environment, processes, and performance, resulting in a sustainable competitive advantage.

Business transformation can be also be likened to the metamorphosis of a caterpillar becoming a butterfly. The butterfly started as a caterpillar, but it cannot stay a caterpillar and still gain the ability to fly. It will have to change. Change is the next logical step. As the caterpillar approaches the time of metamorphosis, certain cells within its body begin to develop; these cells begin the process of building the various parts of the butterfly. The new parts expand and emerge, the old tissue disintegrates, and in a very smooth and ordered way, the caterpillar becomes a butterfly. It stretches its newfound wings and flies away to discover its new landscape.

Transformation and Project Work

What is the relationship between organizational project management (OPM) and business transformation? OPM is the framework that allows organizations to align their operations and projectized resources with strategic goals. Portfolio management, program management, and project management all help ensure project resources are focused on efforts that will best support organizational goals.

- *Portfolio management* is the selection and management of an organization's projects, programs, and operational activities based on numerous key characteristics to achieve specific strategic business objectives. Portfolio management is usually the means by which business transformation is introduced in an organization to achieve results that drive success. The projects selected for the organization's portfolio guide the transformation of the basic organizational structure, realign resources, and keep up with the latest technology.

- *Program management* is the centralized, coordinated management of several related and interdependent projects to achieve the program's strategic objectives and benefits.

- *Project management* is a methodical approach to planning, organizing, and managing project processes to bring about the successful completion of specific project goals and objectives.

- *Program and project management* are usually the means by which business transformation is planned, executed, and controlled to achieve the results for which the initiative was launched.

Business operations also change during the transformation process. Policies are modified; norms and values, reassessed; and systems of service delivery and finance, changed.

Every business must struggle to break through barriers and outmoded attitudes in both the project and operations environments. Behaviors that served us when we were caterpillars are no longer helpful. However, unlike the caterpillar's metamorphosis, business change is not natural. It begins when a company's leadership recognizes that the business cannot stay the same and get different results.

Correctly planned and implemented, business transformation can have far-reaching implications and benefits for the organization, as well as deliver significant results that are visible in the bottom line. Business transformation is a C-level initiative that starts at the top with a CEO mandate. It comprises a variety of competitive strategies impacting the principal elements of a business, consequently resulting in a sustainable competitive advantage (Figure 6-1).[4]

Characteristics of a Business Change	Business Transformation?
CEO-mandated; executive management involved	☑
Primary aspects of business usually impacted	☑
Basis of competition changed	☑
Overall performance enhanced, renewed, and sustained; leadership in marketplace	☑
Drastic increase in market share/market responsiveness	☑

Figure 6-1 Business Transformation Characteristics

Trends Driving Business Transformation

We are reminded every day by the effects of the recession, competition, deregulation, technology, globalization, and mergers and acquisitions that a static business environment is a thing of the past. In a quest to increase the bottom line, executives are being forced to reinvent constantly the way in which they manage and structure their businesses, making transformation the normal state of affairs for most organizations.

When asked to select the external trends that they felt were driving the need for business transformation, 44 percent of respondents cited increased competition from competitors (see Figure 6-2).[5]

The drivers of business transformation can be numerous because businesses may change for a variety of reasons: to regain product quality and market fitness; as a response to a failure; new technology requirements; the ambition to increase competency; a need for improved management and work processes—the list is endless. Here are some questions that can help companies determine whether they need to begin a business transformation:

- Are you reinvesting in opportunities as the market evolves?
- Is your performance superior to that of your major competitors?
- Is your competitive advantage strong enough to attract more customers and more business from existing customers?

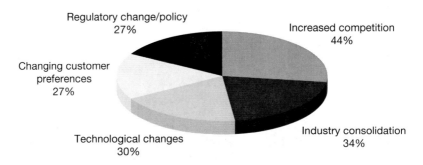

Figure 6-2 Trends Driving Business Transformation

- Are your revenues on target?

- Who is accountable for results?

- What is your organization's strength? Technology? Marketing? Sales? How strong is your business sense?

- Is your company facing heightened competition from domestic and international rivals?

- Are you finding that you need to advertise more to get noticed in the marketplace, but the impact of each advertising dollar spent is decreasing?

- Is your company focused on cutting costs, quality control, and brand management at the expense of growth, innovation, and brand creation?

- Are mergers and acquisitions the principal means by which your company expects to grow?

If you answered yes to a majority of these questions, you need to change your approach. This list represents just some of the questions you can ask, but these can get you started on the path to determining the timing and potential of your organization's transformation. If you don't change, and your competitors *do* change, your business will be in trouble.

The Prevalent Types of Transformation

The past few years in business have been characterized by a succession of fundamental shifts in the way organizations operate and structure themselves. In their search for greater efficiencies, economies of scale, or lower costs, organizations have embraced trends such as outsourcing, off-shoring, and mergers and acquisitions. Although these trends can all have different objectives and require different skills, they are all examples of business transformation.

Meanwhile, rapid technological development has transformed the way information is shared and communicated and the way business processes and transactions are conducted. In 2007, Capgemini Consulting conducted a study on the most prevalent types of business transformation projects undertaken by organizations.[6] Figure 6-3 shows the results of the study.

Transformational Organizations

We will now examine seven transformational organizations—JetBlue, Walmart, General Electric, Barnes & Noble and Borders, Curves, and Apple. While these organizations undertook very different initiatives, they all focused intensively on doing what businesses are supposed to do: make profit, sustain it, and grow it. The scale of the impact of these changes qualifies them as business transformations.

JetBlue

JetBlue, the seventh-largest passenger air carrier in the United States, was founded in 1998. It has a fleet of 297 aircraft and operates more than

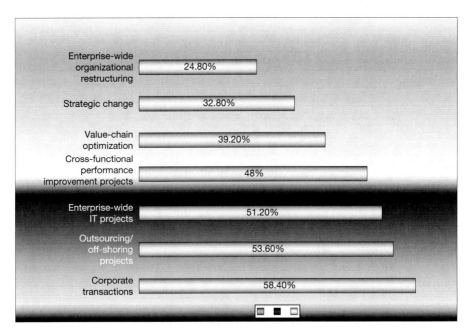

Figure 6-3 Types of Business Transformation Projects

600 daily flights in 19 states, Puerto Rico, Mexico, and five countries in the Caribbean and Latin America. JetBlue transformed its operations by implementing a new network strategy project that focused on putting airplanes where the company could maximize its unit revenues (revenue per available seat mile).[7]

This project enhanced JetBlue's IT systems so that they could handle the tremendous volume and complexity of data the airline now requires. As a connection to the network strategy project, JetBlue also implemented an operational integrity program that improved planning, action, and communication. Currently JetBlue's strategy, execution, culture, customer service, and success are among the most impressive in the travel industry.[8] This transformation project allowed JetBlue to offer low fares while delivering high-quality service to its travelers. The commendable customer service and pricing led to customer loyalty, which was reflected in its profits.

Walmart

Walmart is known for promising low prices. It consistently puts competitors out of business, and its sales exceed the gross national profit of some countries. Walmart sells the very same products or services as other large retailers, but by using differentiated processes, techniques, and materials. Walmart outperforms the competition (and itself). One of the ways it has achieved this is by implementing an industry best practice called cross-docking, a process by which goods from suppliers are trucked to a distribution center and immediately transferred to trucks bound for stores without ever being placed into storage. Cross-docking innovations led to lower inventory levels and lower operating costs, which Walmart translated into lower prices.[9]

General Electric

General Electric (GE) is admired for its ability to drive change through the ranks and was named America's most admired company by *Fortune* magazine six times in the past decade.[10] Today, GE is considered a leader in its industry, but it had to force itself to change to get there. GE embarked upon business transformation to revitalize its business model. Its transformation didn't result in a new product or service; rather, it impacted the way GE produced a product or service. Its restructuring focused on the revenue- and value-creation processes by making a basic change throughout the organization and reinventing existing processes to drive value creation. It produced the same products and provided the same services using different processes, techniques, and materials.[11]

During its transformation, GE discovered that it was focused on the cost side of its businesses, not on its revenue-generating processes. It then embarked on one of the most ambitious digitization projects in the world. This led to record-breaking profits that shifted the ratio of front-office to back-office resources from 60:40 to 90:10, thereby increasing the resources that went directly into revenue-generating activities.[12]

Barnes & Noble and Borders

Barnes & Noble and Borders superstores in the United States underwent a transformation to redefine the scope of the services they offered. The companies realized that hundreds of bookstores were focused solely on the moment a customer purchases a book. Rather than do the same, they asked themselves, "What do customers do before, during, and after purchasing a book?" They found that before purchasing books, buyers like to sit and browse through several selections before making a choice, yet traditional bookstores did not offer a place to do so. In fact, they discouraged the practice. Also, Barnes & Noble and Borders observed that after purchasing books or magazines, customers often went to coffee shops to spend some time alone reading. With these insights, they transformed the product they sell: from books themselves to the pleasure of reading and intellectual exploration. The retailers added lounges and coffee bars and hired knowledgeable staff to create an environment that celebrates reading and learning. In less than six years, Barnes & Noble and Borders emerged as the two largest bookstore chains in the United States, with some 1,300 superstores between them.[13]

Curves

At its inception, the Curves fitness center company was thought to be entering an oversaturated market. However, since 1995, Curves has grown and acquired more than two million members in more than 6,000 locations, with total revenues exceeding $1 billion.[14]

Curves transformed the fitness industry by unlocking a huge untapped market of women who were struggling and failing to stay in shape. Curves achieved transformation by building on the advantages of two strategic groups in the U.S. fitness industry—traditional health clubs and home exercise programs—and eliminated or reduced everything else. Curves asked, "What makes women either trade up or down between traditional health clubs and home exercise programs?"

The company is able to offer memberships at a lower cost—about $30 a month—than most health clubs because its facilities lack traditional gym accoutrements like weight-lifting machines, food, spas, pools, and even locker rooms, which have been replaced by a few curtained changing areas. Curves' low-cost business model also makes its franchises easy to afford compared with the typical start-up investment of $500,000 to $1 million for traditional health clubs (start-up investments for Curves range from $25,000 to $30,000). This explains why Curves facilities have mushroomed quickly (they can be found in most towns of any size in America). Curves is not competing directly with other health and exercise concepts; it has created its own niche in the fitness industry.[15]

Apple

To drive revenue growth, Apple, the developer of the Macintosh personal computer (PC) line, transformed its business model into a high-end consumer-electronics and services company by launching several transformation projects. In January 2001, the company introduced iTunes software for playing and managing digital music files on the Macintosh; ten months later, Apple launched the first iPod.[16]

Though the iPod won rave reviews, it soon became clear that most people would not discard their Windows PC just to use the best MP3 player on the market. In August of 2002, Apple shifted its strategy and introduced an iPod for Windows, one that positioned the company simultaneously in the PC industry and the consumer electronics industry. The company's line of iPod media players, its iTunes online content store, and its newly launched iPhone mobile handset business made up increasingly large shares of its operations. In early 2008, on the strength of skyrocketing sales in those areas and rebounding sales of Macintosh products, Apple's revenues and its stock price reached record levels.[17]

Key Transformation Practices

One striking element of all seven companies' transformations is that they set themselves apart from the competition by differentiating the way they produced products, provided services, or conducted operations, leading to better customer operations. They introduced business transformation projects and programs to achieve dramatic enterprise-level performance improvement, substantial financial benefits, and long-term sustainability and market leadership, which provided a sustainable competitive advantage.

The Benefits of Business Transformation

Most business transformation initiatives should create a sustainable competitive advantage. Through transformation initiatives, organizations ideally instill in themselves an innovative and agile operating model that builds resilience. They become aligned with a compelling vision. In most cases, they transform themselves into high-performance organizations with a clear direction and execution strategy, ultimately benefiting all stakeholders in the value chain.

Organizations taking up transformational initiatives tune themselves better to an existing market or create a new market. Internally, they promote cross-organizational and functional process improvements by introducing new processes and automation for optimal performance and operational excellence. Transformation, if executed properly, can result in much-needed profitability and sustainability.

Driving Successful Business Transformations

Business transformation must start at the top with a CEO mandate. Strong leadership and the support of senior managers are the most important factors in the long-term success of a business transformation project. Chief executives should begin with the development of a vision, a view of the future that will excite and convert potential followers. CEOs should not just initiate projects; they should also play an active role throughout the project's duration by setting clear objectives and ensuring that the whole organization buys into the vision.

In choosing a person to lead the transformation effort, executive leadership must keep in mind that the best transformation leaders are not ones who dictate their plans, but those who have the capability to formulate a compelling vision, organize and manage the change processes, inspire people with a sense of urgency, and help people bring their own creativity to the project. Leaders that lead successful transformation projects always leave a trail in their industry. They take up transformation as an active strategy. What sets them apart is their *execution* of the strategy.

Barriers to Success

Customers' ever-changing demands, the proliferation of competition, and regulatory and compliance regulations are just some of the issues that contribute to the difficulty of making a business transformation effort successful.[18]

Organizations struggling with people issues may also fail when attempting a transformation. The most frequently cited barrier to success in business transformation is the difficulty of winning over the hearts and minds of employees at all levels of the organization. Other issues, such as gaining local management buy-in, cultural differences, lack of resources, and inadequate project ownership also are common barriers to successful transformation.

The failure of transformation projects can also be traced to a lack of clear goals, a lack of understanding of the need for change, no or poor leadership, no incentive to change, or failure to create a short-term win. Business transformation projects frequently fail because not everyone involved in the process had a clear understanding of what needed to be done and how each goal was going to be achieved before any changes took place.

However, these barriers can be mitigated and possibly avoided by understanding why organizations resist needed change, the process for achieving transformation, and the critical role of leadership in driving the change process in a socially healthy way.

Final Thoughts

As organizations continue to grapple with far-reaching changes in technology, competition, demographics, and business practice, the need to undertake business transformation is likely to remain high on the corporate priority list. Business transformation can be a response to marketplace events or a way to address underperformance. Naturally, it will be the biggest single internal project that a company undertakes.

The transformation process starts when an organization's leaders ask themselves, "If I were the competition, what would I do to put us out of business?" Then they find the answers to this question and act on them before the competition does. Understanding the sources of transformation focuses our attention to the changes an organization needs to achieve transformational results. There is no magic formula for business transformation, and it will mean and encompass different things in different organizations. In general, transformation might mean 1) reinventing, restructuring, or reengineering processes, technology, or the organizational structure to 2) bring about significant changes in product development, order fulfillment, demand fulfillment, customer loyalty, customer satisfaction, business precision, market leadership, ability to change, and organizational learning to 3) produce distinctive products or services.

These transformational changes should be driven by executive management, not by the project management office (PMO). Rather, the PMO should be a facilitator that articulates the challenges and the solutions and drives consensus on funding options. At a minimum, transformation should result in better customer operations, better product operations, and better corporate operations that produce better profits, better return on assets, and better positioning for the future for sustainable competitive advantage. Business transformation can therefore be viewed as a way to foster better performance that results in a sustainable competitive advantage.

Imperatives for Successful Business Transformation

- To achieve improvement, it is important to continuously evaluate the external business environment and assess the need for business transformation on an ongoing basis.

- Ensure that everyone in the organization understands the objectives of the business transformation and what it means for them. The CEO is responsible for providing the necessary context and rationale.

- When ranking projects, base decisions not only on existing portfolio metrics but also on business transformation objectives.

- Develop program and project processes that forecast the attainment of transformation benefits at project review points.

- Direct attention and energy toward implementation, which is the riskiest stage of a business transformation project.

- Executives should initiate business transformation projects and should not take a backseat during implementation; rather, they should continue to play an active role for the duration of the project.

- When evaluating the success of a business transformation project, it is important to look beyond the financials and consider the impact on shareholders, employees, and, above all, customers.

- Leaders must be aware of how cultural differences can affect transformation projects. It is not enough to select only functional experts. It is essential to select team members who are strong communicators and can promote the project and motivate employees.

- Promote an organizational culture that shuns bureaucratic processes. Instead, create an environment in which employees feel empowered to take the initiative and share knowledge.

- Ensure that the structure of the organization is flexible, so that projects can be scaled up or scaled down as needed. This requires the development of people who can manage change, are good at multitasking, and can be moved from one project to another without losing focus.

Notes

1 Abe Gubegna (1974), as quoted in Gary Cohen, "If I were the competition, what would I do to put us out of business?" *Newsletter CO2Partners – Executive Coaching Minneapolis, Minnesota* (November 10, 2006). Available online at http://www.co2partners.com/november.htm#article (accessed February 19, 2010).

2 Gary Cohen, "If I were the competition, what would I do to put us out of business?" *Newsletter CO2Partners – Executive Coaching Minneapolis, Minnesota* (November 10, 2006). Available online at http://www. co2partners.com/november.htm#article (accessed February 19, 2010).

3 Ibid.

4 Hema Prem and George Mathew, "Defining Business Transformation," *CuttingEdge* (May 2006), 3.

5 Capgemini Consulting, "Trends in Business Transformation: A study by Capgemini Consulting, in collaboration with The Economist Intelligence Unit" (June 26, 2007). Available online at http://74.125.113.132/search?q=cache:u5l5yL_3iksJ:www.capgemini.com/insights-and-resources/by-publication/trends_in_business_transformation/+trends+in+business+transformation&cd=3&hl=en&ct=clnk&gl=us (accessed February 19, 2010).

6 Ibid.

7 Stephanie Overby, "JetBlue Skies Ahead," *CIO Magazine*, July 1, 2002. Available online at http://www.cio.com/article/31175/JetBlue_Skies_Ahead (accessed January 27, 2010).

8 Ibid.

9 Michael Hammer, "Deep Change: How Operational Innovation Can Transform Your Company," *Harvard Business Review Onpoint Article*, April 1, 2004.

10 Geoffrey Colvin, "What Makes GE Great?" *Fortune*, February 22, 2006. Available online at http://money.cnn.com/2006/02/21/magazines/fortune/mostadmired_fortune_ge/index.htm (accessed September 12, 2009).

11 Ibid.

12 Ibid.

13 W. Chan Kim and Renee Mauborgne, *Blue Ocean Strategy: How to Create Uncontested Market Space and Make the Competition Irrelevant* (Boston: Harvard Business School Press, 2005).

14 Ibid.

15 Ibid.

16 David Yoffie and Michael Slind, "Apple Inc., 2008," *Harvard Business Review Case Study*, February 29, 2008.

17 Jane Black, "Where 'Think Different' Is Taking Apple," *BusinessWeekOnline*, August 2003. Available online at http://www.businessweek.com/technology/content/aug2003/tc2003085_3215_tc112.htm (accessed February 19, 2010).

18 U.S. Department of Defense, *The Business Transformation Toolkit*, version 1.0 (2001), 3.

CHAPTER 7

The Effect of Culture on Projects

Abdur Rafay Badar, PMP

Are you a business leader who manages cross-cultural teams? Are you confident that you hire people who can effectively manage project teams composed of people from different cultures? Or are there too many people-related conflicts in your project portfolio?

In this chapter, you will discover how understanding cultural issues will improve your organizational performance. You will gain insight into:

- Organizational culture and its impact on project work
- What happens when leaders overlook culture
- Using cultural data to improve project delivery
- Aligning culture with organizational strategy.

Three primary colors make up millions of compound colors. The culture of a global organization is similar to one of these compound colors. A unique color is made—or a culture is built—when people from varied backgrounds with different norms, values, beliefs, attitudes, habits, and preferences gather together to accomplish a common organizational or project goal.

According to *Merriam-Webster's Collegiate Dictionary*, *culture*, as it pertains to organizations, is "the set of shared attitudes, values, goals, and practices that characterizes a company or corporation."[1] Successful leaders understand the art of aligning culture with organizational goals. One way to accomplish this is to incorporate an understanding of the complexities of culture when building project teams.

Projects support an organization's strategy by delivering macro-organizational strategies at the project level. By aligning projects and strategy, successful leaders make organizations both effective and efficient. Some experts believe that culture should be another top imperative for leaders. In his book *Good to Great*, Jim Collins asserts that getting the right people in the right roles is the first step, and then creating strategy is the second step.[2]

The Changing Project Environment

Once dominated by the West, the business world is now heavily influenced by rapid growth in Asia. This shift demands that leaders operate in areas of the world they may know little about. They may no longer be able to conduct business the same way they always have. Several trends have emerged in response to the globalization of business and the accompanying cultural changes:

- Virtual teams are pervasive.
- A start-up company can quickly become a multinational company.
- Companies are being pushed to adopt corporate social responsibility.
- Organizations are shifting from outsourcing to multi-sourcing.

Working with people from around the world also means that there is a greater need to embrace diversity and inclusion. *Diversity*, in this context, means all the ways in which our norms, rituals, and values differ. *Inclusion* means how our organizations value those differences. Leaders must be mindful of cultural differences and sensitivities whether interactions are between different business units, different organizations, a consortium of companies, or different regions of the world. For practical reasons alone, leaders must be culturally aware to understand the nuances of cross-cultural communication. For example, a handshake in the United States can mean finalization of an agreement, while a handshake in the Middle East may mean the willingness to negotiate further.

What do diversity and inclusion have to do with projectized work? Project management practices have become more prevalent in the corporate world as organizations continue to segregate ongoing operational activities from nonoperational, one-time project efforts. This gives an organization's people an opportunity to become familiar with and understand cultural requirements during project work, as well as the cultural impact of the products of project work, before handing it over to operations.

While project culture should align upward to the long-term business objectives, the organizational culture must align downward so that resources can be used efficiently, maximizing profitability. At the same time, outcomes from projects are carefully analyzed to adjust organizational strategy and future project objectives. Senior project sponsors are accountable to the organization's board and must make sure projects are successful.

Understanding Individual Behavior

As leaders, our goal is to make sure our projects' outcomes contribute to the organization's strategic interest. Even if your project planning is impeccable, all the project constraints are perfectly balanced, and you have full support from your sponsor, you still need the right environment to support your project. Group dynamics can be controlled by matching the deliverable requirements with competent, committed people and defining the rules of engagement in the project team charter. Consciously supporting desired behaviors and discouraging undesirable behavior from the onset of the project can help create a culture of performance.

The Myers-Briggs Type Indicator® (MBTI) is a personality assessment tool that is useful for determining project team members' and stakeholders' preferences and orientation on four dimensions:

- *Sensing/intuiting:* How does the project stakeholder perceive (gather information)?

- *Judging/perceiving:* How does the project stakeholder deal with data?

- *Thinking/feeling:* How does the project stakeholder make decisions?

- *Introversion/extroversion:* How does the project stakeholder find solutions?

Determining how best to engage project stakeholders will facilitate communications. An introverted sensing project manager communicates differently than an extroverted intuitive sponsor. As part of the stakeholder analysis, the MBTI can be used to match the needs of the job with the style of the client.

Understanding Organizational Behavior

One of the best studies on culture was performed by Geert Hofstede between 1967 and 1973.[3] Hofstede analyzed data on the values of 100,000 IBM employees in 50 countries. He determined that within societies (and organizations), there are four cultural dimensions. Hofstede added a fifth dimension after conducting another international study with a new survey instrument, the Chinese Value Survey. The five dimensions, which should be considered when managing project work, include:

1. Power distance index (PDI): Describes the degree of inequality between people.

2. Individualism (IDV): Describes the importance one gives to individuality over group conformance.

3. Masculinity (MAS): Describes the degree to which the traditional male role—which combines achievement, control, and power—is supported.

4. Uncertainty avoidance (UAI): Describes the tolerance of uncertainty and ambiguity in the society.

5. Long-term orientation (LTO): Degree to which a society looks forward when making decisions.

Later, similar research conducted elsewhere found a strong correlation with Hofstede's dimensions.[4]

Once an organization's leadership has taken a "culture snapshot" of the organization using a tool like Hofstede's survey, they must update the organization's performance measurement system to reinforce desirable behaviors and discourage deviant behaviors. This also means that the organization has to determine what kind of culture it wants to encourage. Leaders can use Hofstede's survey to find ways to measure and influence employees':

- Willingness to collaborate
- Tolerance of failure
- Adaptability.

By understanding behavior and our organization's culture, we can determine who to include in the project team, how to influence others, and how to resolve conflict.

Culture in Practice

How do we mix all of the elements of projectized work to align organizational strategy? We would like to create a team and an environment that is fit for the project, with a focus on long-term organizational goals. While the team's actions should align to project success, leadership behavior must align to portfolio success.

For a construction project to build a power plant in Dubai, United Arab Emirates (UAE), our project delivery organization understood the importance of getting the right people in the right roles in the client's organization. The project had a rough start; the original consortium partner missed deadlines. That original partner, who was in charge of civil and mechanical construction, was new to the industry. In contrast, our knowledge of the client's organizational culture—an environment infested with micromanagers and plagued by interdepartmental conflicts affecting project scope, quality, and risks—made it clear that our delivery organization had to appoint a project manager with the cultural and emotional maturity to handle the complexity of this project.

The project manager immediately appointed an acceleration team to be present onsite. The acceleration team was charged with finding alternatives, guiding the civil and mechanical contractor, and negotiating contracts. The project management team focused its attention on:

- The project's success
- People
- Profitability.

Focusing on these project variables allowed our project team to align our client's strategy with project success.

We accelerated project success by focusing on finding creative solutions to make the system operational before the summer began; summer temperatures in Dubai sometimes exceed 122°F. The new project team found solutions to the mechanical and civil problems and successfully completed the system before summer. The project team focused on the needs of the client and gained buy-in on its acceleration strategy. They went beyond the contract requirements to make sure the time constraint was met.

Beyond simply completing the project work, the project team built an atmosphere of respect and trust. Even though the project team spent more money up front on acceleration efforts—e.g., more experts onsite, workarounds, increased onsite and back-office coordination—it improved the client's perception of the delivery organization. The team managed communication and conflicts onsite and positioned all decisions in the context of the end goal.

The project manager was both responsible and accountable, and the whole team cooperated to meet the changing demands of the project. In addition, the project manager was sensitive to the cultural reasons for project success.

- *Central control:* The mix of the client's culture and the consortium culture required tight control of the project. The project manager frequently visited the site to make sure that conflicts were aired and discussed. This created a "discuss and decide" atmosphere, which was very different from the previous project environment in which the client had to function as an "error detective."

- *Engagement of sponsor:* The project manager used his power as a senior member of the delivery organization to gain access to the real project sponsor. In the countries of the Gulf Cooperation Council (Saudi Arabia, UAE, Bahrain, Qatar, Kuwait, Oman, and Yemen), sponsors are seldom available and rely largely on the consultants. This means that a company's relationship with the contractor is through a trusted middleman. Gaining access to the sponsor positively influenced the collaboration between all parties.

- *Project team performance:* By regaining control of the project and engaging the sponsor, the project team was carefully protected from negative and distracting political influences and was able to finish its activities without disturbance. The client's "detectives," the fault finders, were held in check because the project team followed fixed quality standards and protocols. Because the client's engineers were too sensitive to deviate from scope and specification, tight control on the information ensured central control as well. The difference between the sponsor's requirements and those of the engineers made managing the project a challenge. Acceleration efforts were made to address the sponsor's needs, but communications were directed toward the engineers. The project manager made it clear that the team could finish the work faster if the client showed flexibility on the other constraints. This established a culture of trade-offs right at the site.

By making sure it met deadlines before contractual penalties set in, the team bought senior management support. Not only did the project manager meet his financial milestones at a time when his company really needed to, but he also gained the confidence of the client. The project team also influenced the consultant's and the client's teams to accomplish project objectives by taking risks like redesigning, fast-tracking, and increasing spending to reach the schedule milestones. Taking risks paid off. The client officially declared this to be its best project.

When balancing projects, people, and profitability, the culture of all the performing parties must be considered. Putting pressure on the project team to comply without cultural sensitivity is like walking a tightrope without a safety net below.

Can You Afford to Overlook Culture?

In the last 20 years, much research has been done on the subject of culture and organizational success. While there is no guarantee that a particular culture will produce good results, there definitely is evidence that "good companies have found good culture," says Riaz Siddiqui, founder and managing partner of Denham Capital in Houston.

Former Siemens AG CEO Klaus Kleinfeld did not find good culture. His tenure at Siemens ended with painful results. Kleinfeld had successfully restructured Siemens AG in Germany, and within two years, it attained one of the highest sales revenue and profits in the industry.[5] But he failed to work with Betriebsrat, the German giant's powerful workers council, or to adapt to the company's culture of loyalty. In May 2007 Kleinfeld was replaced.

Did cultural factors in Germany have something to do with Kleinfeld's dismissal? Let's look at some of the data from Hofstede's study of cultural dimensions. Figure 7-1 shows Hofstede's data on the five dimensions of culture for the United States and Germany.[6]

Country	PDI	IDV	MAS	UAI	LTO
United States	40	91	62	46	29
Germany	35	67	66	65	31

Figure 7-1 Geert Hofstede's Cultural Dimension
Scores for the United States and Germany

The individualism (IDV) and uncertainty avoidance (UAI) scores, shed light on the cultural differences between Germany and the United States. U.S. society was ranked the highest of all countries surveyed in the individualism dimension, indicating a society in which people have loose bonds with others. This is in contrast to the score for Germany, which indicates more interconnectedness. The other major difference is in the countries' outlook on uncertainty. The Germans scored higher on this dimension, indicating that in Germany, decisions are made with prudence.

This gives some insight into the challenges Kleinfeld had to face during his tenure in Germany. While his years of corporate experience in the United States helped him push Siemens AG's revenues higher, it failed to prepare him for the cultural sensitivity needed to engage the interdependent, loyal, and forward-thinking German workforce.

Organizational project leaders must be mindful of the cultural needs of their project portfolios. Let's further define culture. Organizational culture—"the way we do things around here"—is composed of rituals and values. *Rituals*, or processes, are ordered sequences established and followed by the community. They are relatively easier to change than values.

Changes to rituals, however closely held these rituals were in the past, can be instituted by:

• Adjusting the project prioritization system

• Changing management methodology (best practices).

Values, which are concerned with ethics and morals, are closer to the core of the company and are more resistant to change. Changing them may take a long time and may require:

- Adjusting the reporting structure
- Changing the performance management system
- Hiring the right people.

Leaders mindful of rituals and values in their environment can steer their companies toward success.

- Toyota did it by focusing on "soft" areas such as *chie*—learning from experience—in addition to "hard" innovations such as the Toyota Production System, which decentralized decision-making.[7]
- Nucor did it by aligning bonuses with performance across the board and creating a no-corner-office environment in which senior executives deemphasize their titles.[8]
- Sony did it by transforming its culture into an innovation culture influenced by its creative founders Akio Morita and Ibuka.[9]
- IBM accomplished it by shifting from a proprietary product-based business to a service business.[10]

All these companies worked on their values to transform their organizational culture. This is difficult and may take a long time, but it's possible.

What project-related problems occur if you overlook organizational culture?

- Loss of opportunities to create a team culture of trust
- Inability to create successful partnerships with all stakeholders
- Lack of alignment of team resources to project priorities
- A focus on short-term goals while potentially sacrificing long-term goals.

Despite widespread use of project management principles, the industry is still full of examples of failed projects. According to research done by

Business Improvement Architects (BIA), in Canada, culture is the missing ingredient. BIA has developed a change management system called Project Culture Initiative™, which focuses on ensuring strong practices in the following areas:

- Reporting structures
- Project prioritization
- Performance measurement systems.[11]

BIA's conclusion is that the right culture will ensure that leaders are actively involved, conflicts are resolved, teams are motivated, and work is done effectively and efficiently. Leaders need to understand the current and upcoming challenges related to performance.

Culture and Work Performance

There is a strong correlation between low project management maturity and poorly performing cultures. Consider a project with team members from nine different countries. The team is composed of direct employees, freelancers, vendors, and subcontractors. The team's job is to produce a plan for a complex project. Let's suppose the following environmental factors exist:

- The project budget and deadlines have already been given to the team.
- The project manager wants the plan to fit into the time and cost constraints.
- The project members are not encouraged to communicate.
- Bad news is not welcomed.
- The steering committee/management team is rarely available.
- No formal reward or penalty mechanisms exist.

In such a situation, a flawed culture will develop in just a few weeks. Unfortunately, project environments like this one are not uncommon.

What happens when an organization with a troubled culture adds multiple projects to its portfolio without recognizing that its project practices can't support more work? This happens often in organizations that do not have mature project management practices.

Overcoming Challenges to Transform Company Culture

A culture of trust, openness, and mutual enrichment is required if an organization is to produce great and lasting results. Some organizations' cultures do not resemble this ideal at all. Someone may need to pull the people in these organizations out of Plato's cave. (The allegory of the cave, in Plato's *Republic*, describes the predicament of mankind: believing our own point of view to be correct, regardless of reality.)[12] Plato explains that reality can be discovered only through an intellectual search. So project teams need a more knowledgeable outsider who can reveal to them the reality of their organization, as if from a higher elevation. Coming out of the cave brings project stakeholders closer to reality and allows them to fix a flawed culture, which has a meaningful and positive effect on the organization.

An initiative to assess and improve project practices is an opportunity for organizations to transform the way things are done. Who should own this initiative? Senior leadership must realize that the current environment does not support the organization's needs and must formally address the environmental factors that prevent the organization from succeeding. They need to articulate what must change; they are responsible for suggesting that people must be pulled out of the cave. Project senior leaders, managers, and sponsors of change initiatives can articulate what cultural changes are needed to make organizations better. Failure to manage and support the behavioral change needed to support the transformation can be fatal.

Organizational leaders face four primary challenges as they work to transform company cultures: overcoming the compliance mentality, managing subcultures, establishing an identity and a clear vision, and standing tall amidst environmental changes.

Overcoming the Compliance Mentality

It is more imperative than ever to ensure that your culture doesn't interfere with your organization's ability to execute strategy. Why? Part of the reason lies in the new challenges organizations now face. The business world has been shaken by the recent economic downturn and worldwide corporate scandals. There is more pressure on companies to be socially responsible and to have transparent business practices and better ethical and moral values. When leaders transform their organizations' culture, they often prioritize ethics and compliance.

Unfortunately, laws regarding compliance can be very complex and ambiguous. Insistence on compliance unleashes "compliance sharks" in the murky corporate world. An emphasis on compliance also conflicts with the need for fast-paced change.

What forces organizations toward increased compliance? Generally, in good times organizations relax, and in bad times they shift toward tight governance. Balancing compliance requirements and the flexibility needed for innovation and problem-solving should be considered on a strategic level. Layered on top of this conflict is the fact that during an improvement effort, operations or project performance goes down. It is only when the transformation is complete that you see the real benefit: the capabilities or results of the improvement initiative.

To illustrate, let's say that a section of highway is being extended. The construction contractor has to cordon off half of the highway during the course of the project. During this period, there will be even more traffic congestion than before. The benefit of the improvement is realized only once the extension is finished and the new section is operational. When working to institute cultural changes, you must be mindful of the challenges the transitional period will bring. The cultural lessons learned from projects should be used to improve future projects.

Managing Subcultures

Organizations comprise different functional and projectized units. Each of these units has a subculture. A unit in charge of project delivery may have a different culture from the unit responsible for research and development or the unit responsible for corporate planning. Management should make sure that each subculture is appropriate for its area of operation and that together, they all add up to define a portfolio culture or a desirable organizational culture.

Organizational project management addresses how to bridge operations and projects. Cultural elements such as rituals and values exist for a historical reason. Effective organizational project management therefore includes understanding each organizational unit's stakeholder culture, then crafting strategies to mitigate rituals or values that lead to poor performance or otherwise negatively influence projects.

Establishing an Identity and a Clear Vision

All organizations that survive have a common ideology, a body of ideas, an identity. Organizations have to know their core business and stick to it. Without this, they are lost. (We can draw parallels between organizations and highly organized animals such as ants and bees that display—and need—control and integration.)

Clear corporate identity statements or corporate mission and vision statements answer essential questions and define connections between strategies and projects. Management consultant Lynn A. Walker asserts that "one of the key requirements to establishing an identity is self-confidence. [For example,] it takes self-confidence to turn down a potential customer. It takes even more self-confidence to allow employees three levels down from the chief executive to turn down non-customers. It takes an even higher level of confidence to *demand* that they turn down non-customers."[13] Confidence is a cultural trait, not a technical process.

In today's corporate world, where mergers and acquisitions are so common, how do leaders resolve the differences in identity and culture clash that two different organizational units may have? Having a sound vision will clarify "what we do and don't do around here." Knowing what you do and what you don't do defines the organization's ethical and moral boundaries. These two elements build confidence in an organization and help projects more successfully deliver results to operations. Everyday decision-making becomes easier, and there is less conflict between senior leaders and the project team.

Standing Tall Amidst Environmental Changes

Organizations do not operate in a vacuum. They are impacted by external factors not in their control. Therefore, an organization's culture must be one that helps it adapt quickly to environmental changes. Empirical evidence links organizational culture and financial performance, and the ability to adapt fast is certainly associated with organizational excellence.[14]

Organizational project management requires a tool to gauge organizational agility—in other words, how quickly your culture can adapt to outside factors without compromising its core values. Consider an airplane in flight. Its speed, ailerons, elevators, and rudder constantly adjust to keep the airplane on a defined path. The engine adjusts the thrust when needed. In an organization, a positive culture is the thrust that keeps the employees and teams motivated amid changing environmental conditions. Corporate identity defines the path, and diversity and inclusion provide the correction needed to keep the organization on course. Diversity offers multiple perspectives, and inclusion enables leaders to form a comprehensive solution.

Developing a Cultural Plan

Because organizations are (or should be) vision-oriented—that is, their focus is on survival and growth in the future—they must concentrate on cultural development. Culture should be in the front of organizational leaders' minds.

A high-performance team culture is one in which all members, including subcontractors, vendors, and freelancers, work seamlessly toward a common goal. Old and mature organizations develop a personality, which is referred to as if it were a real person. For example, during negotiations with a strategic procurement team from 162-year-old Siemens, it was striking to hear "Yes, we understand your point, but Siemens won't do it." This alignment of people with the company is typical in mature organizations like General Electric, Sony, and Tata. Leaders must envision the character of their company and devise a hiring strategy that works toward this vision.

An organizational project management perspective, which is all about how projects can deliver greater value to operations or to customers, has much to offer to general management. Lessons learned, tested, and proven during project work can be adapted for the organization as a whole. In a sense, project work offers a simulation environment for cultural issues, helping the organization build a performance improvement culture that is needed for the growth of the organization.

In Brief

Three steps can facilitate cultural strategic alignment at the project level:

1. Determine the cultural values that affect a project goal or long-term strategy. Such values may be discerned from the project charter, policies, guidelines, procedures, checklists, human resource communications, and process flows.

2. Use project performance assessment tools to evaluate outcomes from step 1.

3. Work to eliminate the negative factors affecting business outcomes and enhance the positive factors using information from steps 1 and 2.

Notes

1 Merriam-Webster Online Dictionary, "culture," http://www.merriam-webster.com/dictionary/culture (accessed March 1, 2010).

2 Jim Collins, *Good to Great: Why Some Companies Make the Leap … and Others Don't* (New York: HarperCollins, 2001).

3 Geert Hofstede, Geert Hofstede™ Cultural Dimensions, http://www.geert-hofstede.com (accessed February 1, 2010).

4 For more information on organizational culture, see Geert Hofstede and Gert Jan Hofstede, *Cultures and Organizations: Software of the Mind* (New York: McGraw Hill, 2004).

5 Jack Ewing, "Siemens' Culture Clash," *Business Week*, January 29, 2007. Online at http://www.businessweek.com/magazine/content/07_05/b4019058.htm (accessed March 1, 2010).

6 Geert Hofstede, Geert Hofstede™ Cultural Dimensions, http://www.geert-hofstede.com (accessed February 1, 2010).

7 Hirotaka Takeuchi, Emi Osono, and Norihiko Shimizu, "The Contradictions That Drive Toyota's Success," *Harvard Business Review*, June 2008. Online at http://hbr.org/2008/06/the-contradictions-that-drive-toyotas-success/ar/1 (accessed March 1, 2010).

8 Jim Collins, *Good to Great: Why Some Companies Make the Leap … and Others Don't* (New York: HarperCollins, 2001).

9 Akio Morita, Edwin M. Reingold, Mitsuko Shimomura, *Made in Japan: Akio Morita and Sony* (New York: Signet, 1988).

10 Free Encyclopedia of Ecommerce, "IBM Corp- Early History, Move to Computing, Shift to E-business Services," http://ecommerce.hostip.info/pages/562/IBM-Corp.html (accessed March 1, 2010).

11 For more information on the Project Culture Initiative™, see Business Improvement Architects, "Undertaking a Project Culture Initiative™." Online at www.bia.ca/pci-coaching.htm (accessed March 1, 2010).

12 Wikipedia, "Allegory of the Cave," http://en.wikipedia.org/wiki/Allegory_of_the_cave (accessed February 1, 2010).

13 Lynn A. Walker, "Create an Identity," Boundary Management Consulting, http://www.boundarymanagement.com/Create%20an%20Identity.htm (accessed February 1, 2010).

14 John P. Kotter and James L. Heskett, *Corporate Culture and Performance* (New York: Free Press, 1992), 7–8.

CHAPTER 8

Performing Assessments that Dramatically Improve Business Results

Sara Núñez, PMP, OPM3® Assessor/Consultant

What do your organization or your customers think about your project, program, and portfolio processes? Are the processes known for getting the right things done? Do the practices drive your organization to gain competitive advantages in the market? These are key questions asked by any organization effectiveness and efficiency expert. They are especially important questions to ask service delivery organizations, because their project, program, or portfolio practices represent their company's product, brand, and success in the market. There is no room for failure in these practices when they support engagements that bring in revenue to sustain and improve business results.

In this chapter, we will look at assessments that deliver organizational improvement. In particular, we are going to study a project assessment that delivered significant business results in a service delivery organization. In this chapter, you will find:

- A case study of a successful project environment assessment
- Key practices that support project environment assessments.

The Value of Assessments

Unstable economic conditions drive business leaders to align their organizational missions and models to current conditions. A project environment assessment can facilitate such alignment efforts. Most organizations require changes—immediately.

As an organizational effectiveness and efficiency expert, I have worked with many global corporations over the last 25 years implementing organizational processes that enable improved business results. In this chapter, I share the keys to the success of my approach.

The first is moving from a solution approach to a results approach. I look at the organizational enablers—the components of people, processes, and tools an organization uses to perform a job. That's where most assessments stop. The key to assessments that deliver big results is identifying the linkage of organizational enablers to the results most needed by an organization.

Next, I answer the question of why those people, processes, and tools aren't getting the expected results. There are many reasons. We look at each component again and evaluate its effectiveness and approach. Lasting organizational improvement comes from understanding the reasons organizational components are or are not working.

This chapter presents a proven plan for assessing the environment in which project work is performed and creating a path for organizational and project management success. The project environment assessment process includes eight steps:

1. Confirm the reasons for change.
2. Determine the change objectives.
3. Plan and perform an assessment.
4. Design an improvement solution.
5. Plan the change.

6. Implement the change.

7. Monitor and control the change.

8. Re-assess and continue improving.

This is a proven process. I have used this approach in many organizations in multiple industries and on several continents. This is a practical approach adapted from best practices from key industry maturity models. It can be used by any organization that needs to improve the effectiveness of its organizational project management practices and improve business performance.

The case covered in this chapter focuses on an organization in Latin America that needed to increase customer satisfaction and move into an industry leadership position. The organization followed this eight-step project environment assessment model, and the results were impressive:

- Projects' cycle time was reduced significantly (e.g., a previous project lasting 12 months was now reduced to 3 months on a comparable project).
- Projects' return on investment improved by 67 percent.

Next, I explain how to get these impressive results.

A Project Environment Assessment Model

This project environment assessment model (Figure 8-1) is an effective catalyst for both project and organizational improvements. It is a problem-solving approach that provides the necessary framework to create rapid and positive change. This assessment works by:

- Focusing on identifying organizational reasons to change—in other words, the problem(s)
- Tracing the root causes of the problem(s)
- Creating practical and effective project solutions.

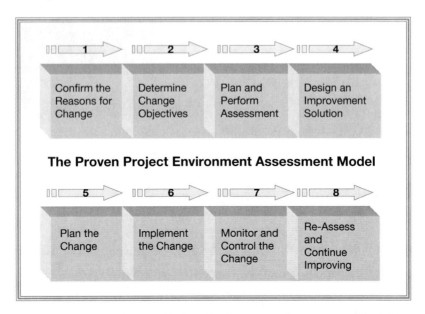

Figure 8-1 The Proven Project Environment Assessment Model

This assessment provides a detailed end-to-end process that implements changes in your organization that will drive real business results. Unlike many other project assessments, this is not an isolated, standalone project management-practices assessment. This project environment assessment creates deep linkages between organizational challenges and the alignment of projectized work to strategic needs.

Step 1: Confirm the Reasons for Change

Organizations must solve the right problem or problems to get better results. However, many leaders make assumptions about what is broken. They fund improvement initiatives and then expectations aren't met.

To avoid that situation, we help organizations understand their desired end state and how their project, program, and portfolio processes can enable them to meet their goals. We look at the overall portfolio of projects and programs the organization has selected. We keep asking, "Why are the current goals important? Are those goals and business objectives still realistic? Are you selecting the right projects to meet your goal? Which processes are most important to your success, and why do you believe that?"

Organizations need a clear picture of the environmental reasons that demand change. Assessment initiatives usually seek ways to improve business performance or reduce operational costs by creating new processes and improving existing processes. This requires us to identify the factors that will threaten:

- Products
- Profits
- Processes
- Corporate values.

I can do this either at the highest level of an organization or for an individual business unit or division. This is the critical first step that focuses on identifying the need for change.

Key Practices

It is important to initiate your analysis by viewing your organization from an end-to-end, strategy-to-projects perspective. Ensure an end-to-end approach by:

- Involving key leaders
- Reviewing the performance of your products and services portfolios
- Reviewing customer-satisfaction scorecards
- Reviewing operations metrics
- Ensuring that dissent during discussion is heard
- Reaching general agreement by the end of the discussion.

Gaining agreement about the challenges the organization faces with regard to its overall performance is critical to setting the stage for a successful project environment assessment.

Case Study

I used this process during a recent engagement with PayRoll Sociedad Anonima (PayRoll S.A.), a software service organization. The CEO of PayRoll S.A., Rodrigo Castro, and his staff recognized a need to change their organization. In 2007, PayRoll S.A. planned to attract more shareholders to increase funding to grow its business. It was absolutely critical for Castro to ensure that his organization could reach these goals. When the leadership of PayRoll S.A. met, they identified the following business challenges and needs (Figure 8-2):

	External Challenges/Needs		Internal Challenges/Needs
1	Improve corporate image	1	Reduce cost
2	Improve customer satisfaction	2	Increase profit
3	Improve quote to cash	3	Improve the work environment
4	Improve on-time delivery	4	Implement project governance
5	Increase client base	5	Improve employee satisfaction
6	Attract larger clients	6	Improve cross-functional work

Figure 8-2 PayRoll Sociedad Anonima Business Challenges and Needs

Lesson

Meet with key organizational leaders to gain agreement on urgent drivers for change.

Step 2: Determine Change Objectives

There are many important business objectives, including increasing revenue, reducing cost, and improving productivity. But these objectives have unintended conflicts, and there is explicit competition for funding. In step 1, management focused on determining which of the organization's objectives support the improvement of business results. In step 2, these objectives are prioritized. Prioritization drives what must happen to get to the desired organization end state. Prioritization is important for several reasons:

- Some objectives accelerate achieving results
- Prioritization drives the customization of the assessment.

The objectives an organization chooses can be related to corporate strategy, operations, or projects, programs, or portfolios. The goal is to select objectives that will boost projects' ability to improve organizational results.

Key Practices

The organization must perform an insightful analysis of its financial performance. If, for example, your business is missing targets and performing poorly, you must:

- Review current financial and operational goals
- Review current business assumptions to determine if any have changed
- Assess whether goals are achievable based on the current market situation
- Identify gaps between expected financial goals and current performance
- Determine what needs to be done to optimize the organization's portfolio
- Update business assumptions or create new ones
- Create or update organizational design assumptions for projectized work.

Creating or updating objectives creates new mandates for ongoing operations and for project work.

Case Study

PayRoll S.A.'s main objective for the assessment was to establish a well-defined organization equipped with the best people and best practices to deliver specific business results. The company had to make organizational changes to manage project work more effectively. The company's first step was to hire a results-oriented executive director, Hugo Quevedo, for its project management office. Quevedo had two priorities: to confirm the assumptions provided by the business leaders and to seek help in performing an assessment. He hired Cadence Management Corporation (Cadence), an international project management consulting firm. They worked together to:

- Perform an internal audit to identify the problems
- Interview external clients to understand their frustrations and perspectives
- Propose and prioritize organizational objectives to address the organization's end-state needs.

There were several key findings. PayRoll S.A. was not able to track project cost or profit. Commitment dates were simply guesses. Scope was never defined or documented. The company was wasting time and resources by making many visits to clients' sites, and clients were very unhappy. The internal functional teams were very frustrated with one another.

Lesson

Look at the organizational needs and challenges from step 1 and assess what new objectives are needed for operations or project work to meet the new strategic needs.

Step 3: Plan and Perform an Assessment

Step 1 focused on executive alignment around the reasons to change. The discussions during that stage were focused on how to improve organizational end results. Step 2 prioritized objectives. Step 3 focuses on assessing project maturity.

Maturity assessments align project work to support the needs of an organization. Why do work that shouldn't be done at all? Why improve processes that neither customers nor management values?

Many maturity models have been created by professional and academic groups. Several project management assessment models review both project work and the context in which it is performed. The era of improving only project practices is long gone.

A model that links project work to an organizational context is the *Organizational Project Management Maturity Model* (OPM3®) designed by industry experts at the Project Management Institute (PMI). This model provides a way to evaluate organizational enablers: people and processes tied to project, program, and portfolio management best practices. A PMI-certified OPM3® consultant or assessor can evaluate your organization and determine where people are not using best practices or where best practices are not getting the best results.

Key Practices

The scope of the assessment must be clear. This proven assessment process works backwards, starting with the business reason for the change and the key objectives that must be improved. Urgency is key. Focus on the business leaders' mandate for change. Adjust the scope of the assessment process to ensure that projectized work and all the impacted processes are examined and the relevant stakeholders are included. For rapid results, tailor the assessment to the areas targeted for change.

- Identify assessment scope.
- Validate assessment scope.
- Identify key stakeholders.
- Create an assessment plan.
- Assess people, project processes, and environment.
- Prioritize findings internally.
- Provide results.
- Evangelize the need for change.

This assessment will yield a list of best practices, as well as practices that may be causing poor performance. Provide a complete report of your assessment results to the organization. This report should include an executive summary of the findings, including challenges and key success factors for positive outcomes. It is important to highlight both positive and negative findings. Be objective, and do not sugarcoat the findings. Finally, be prepared to answer any challenges presented by employees.

Case Study

Quevedo worked with Cadence and its local partner, E+PMC, to perform an OPM3® assessment. Cadence asked me, a PMI-certified OPM3® consultant, to lead the combined team. The team's assessment included an analysis of the current situation, including PayRoll S.A.'s existing processes, best practices, skill sets, and organizational enablers.

The consultant team prepared for the assessment and the approval of the scope and initiated a series of interviews with the internal organization and the clients. This assessment provided PayRoll S.A. with specific project management improvement opportunities. The team's preliminary findings addressed PayRoll S.A.'s:

- Strategic plans, business model, and business objectives performance
  - Projects were not delivered on time, causing major impacts on the customers
  - Projects were not validated to confirm strategic alignment to business objectives
- Project processes
  - Very poor or no project planning processes
  - Lack of standardization of documents caused duplication of effort on every project
- Organizational context
  - Very skilled personnel, but employees' roles and responsibilities were unclear
  - No project management vision or policies
  - No performance agreements to define objectives and performance evaluations.

Lesson

The organizational maturity assessment showed the root causes of the performance problems that prevented the organization from meeting its business objectives. The assessment analyzed whether effective practices were in place to support step 1 (confirm reasons for change) and step 2 (determine change objectives) and included detailed information on the findings.

Step 4: Design an Improvement Solution

Assessment results from step 3 will provide executives with enough data to decide whether to fund additional investment in initiatives or projects to improve project, program, or portfolio processes. Many assessments die here, even if the initiative is funded. Why? Because the responsibility for designing a solution can't be fully delegated, either to support staff or to external consultants. Executive engagement is needed to ensure that the solution is designed by politically adept and technically capable individuals. If the assessment results were not relevant, or if the solution design is not agreed to by leaders of the organization, over time the organization will withhold resources or sponsorship.

There must be agreement on how the proposed changes will be implemented. Process improvement is the goal of the assessment, but overcoming organizational resistance to change is equally important during this stage.

Key Practices

The importance of skilled facilitative project leadership cannot be under-estimated.

Leaders must influence and motivate stakeholders to success through shared accountability. Get the correct resources involved. This will dramatically improve the results.

- Identify stakeholders responsible for implementing the change.
- Keep the focus on actions that will fulfill organizational objectives.

- ○ Revalidate the scope of the change initiative with the implementation team.
- ○ Create an implementation plan.
- ○ Prioritize actions that achieve the fastest impact.
- Gain business leaders' approval of the plan.
- Educate all stakeholders to improve the adoption rate.

At this point, you now have approval and commitment for the change!

Case Study

PayRoll S.A. and its project management office (PMO) leader formed a cross-functional team that included subject matter experts from the consulting firm. Together they reviewed the assessment findings, prioritized them, and designed an action plan. They aligned the recommendations to the business objectives identified for this effort.

Lesson

Your organization and external consultants must work together to design solutions that address the problems that are preventing you from meeting your business objectives. The purpose of this team should be to prioritize problems and solutions to guarantee real results. Team accountability and leadership is absolutely necessary for designing the right set of solutions.

Step 5: Plan the Change

Executive buy-in and funding approval is needed before you can create a detailed list of funding sources, acquire talent, and develop a list of milestones. Offering a good solution for the problems or improvement needed in step 4 is valuable; great planning in step 5 is even more valuable. So use the same team from step 4 to plan implementation of the change.

Key Practices

Large changes are risky. Create a road map to determine the timing for implementing the proposed recommendations. Also, assign a sponsor for each change. A project sponsor is critical to support the project.

- Execute the recommendations:
  - Clearly describe the changes, the expected benefits, any new processes, and the implementation strategy.
  - Discuss organizational risks and constraints.
  - Create timelines.
- Ensure that roles and responsibilities for the improvement initiative are clearly delineated.
- Develop clear performance agreements with employees.
- Provide training as part of the performance agreement.
- Work with human resources when organizational design changes are needed—new skill sets or core competencies may be required. This could mean that the organization may have to hire new people or develop the skills of existing personnel.

Case Study

PayRoll S.A. formed an internal team to perform critical functions. With the help of the consultants, the team worked to implement the proposed solution and plan the implementation. They took rapid action, immediately investing in a project management tool that could track projects end-to-end and provided access to clients. They simplified the company's project management methodology by tailoring industry best practices based on key deliverables, project type, and complexity. Also, immediate action was taken to:

- Establish the PMO function and start using the project management methodology and tools
- Establish clear roles and define responsibilities for the PMO organization, the customer, and supporting functions within PayRoll S.A.
- Delegate clear authority to the project managers to become the leaders and representatives of PayRoll S.A. in the eyes of customers
- Design tracking mechanisms
- Identify PMO business and financial objectives

- Secure the budget to hire experienced project managers
- Identify key metrics and reports to track project performance and assess performance with regard to objectives.

Lesson

The right approach to implementing organizational changes and process improvements is critical to the success of your changes. Getting the right stakeholders involved in designing the solution will guarantee buy-in and support. It also creates a team-oriented environment in which failure or success is the responsibility or glory of all. Plan and get approval for the implementation of solutions to ensure rapid business results.

Step 6: Implement the Change

At this point, the organization has a clear idea of the end results it wants and the objectives or metrics it will use to track success. It has performed an assessment to highlights gaps in its capabilities and has created and funded a plan to address those gaps.

Now, the assessment team either works with the organization to implement the plan or transitions the plan to a PMO.

Step 6 requires the affected users to adopt the proposed solution. In reality, this step is concurrent with all of the others. Specific internal resources or consultants can be assigned to influence staff to rapidly adopt the change. Motivate employees to become change agents. Employees must understand and commit to changes, or they will never be fully implemented. The success of your implementation depends on employees' active participation. Step 6 is not complete until the plan is in place and people are acting in accordance with it.

Both top-down communication and horizontal communication are needed to explain changes and the purpose of those changes to the organization. Managers may update performance agreements or yearly performance appraisals to include any required training, new functional responsibilities, and recognition incentives.

Key Practices

- Hold checkpoint meetings with the departments affected by the changes.
- Request feedback and capture reactions to the change.
- Hold coffee meetings or have hallway conversations with people at all levels of the organization.
- Take corrective action as needed.
- Track the completion of your communication, training, and marketing plans. Your communication plan should include the participation of the process owner, sponsors, and any other key stakeholders in weekly staff, quarterly, and annual review meetings.
- Track training completion and ensure 100 percent participation.
- Make sure you have the right support system to answer questions and monitor the implementation.
- Remember that adoption takes time.

Case Study

The changes made by PayRoll S.A. had a significant impact on communication and organizational design. Quevedo staffed the newly created PMO function with project managers and authorized them to lead the projects and to become the main interface with the client. The system engineers also reported to the PMO, which improved their collaboration and communication with the project managers and helped them deliver the best solution to the customer. The PMO function engaged other senior managers and made them accountable for the success or the failure of the organizational changes. The PMO depended on other business operations like IT and marketing to deliver the product according to the customers' specifications. Peer support was gained for this implementation.

Lesson

Step 6 is the most important step and the most difficult one for organizations. This step is complete when the design solution is implemented and all the processes and behaviors in the proposed design solution are in place.

Step 7: Monitor and Control the Change

Now business process owners and their staff are working with the results of the improved processes. Soon executives will ask whether the improvements are helping staff better meet organizational objectives. Step 6, while important, is only the initial implementation of the improved practices. The plan created in step 5 must clearly define the key indicators of the initiative's effectiveness. On an ongoing basis, the organization assigns resources to measure progress and drive necessary corrective action to stimulate better performance.

Key Practices

How can you really measure the effectiveness of an assessment effort? The answer is not simple. Return on investment is important, but each organization needs to create a set of objectives tailored to its individual environment. Key points:

- Track assessment value.
- Project sponsors and key stakeholders should take responsibility for the success of this effort.
- Track and measure the value of implemented changes for any assessment effort and report results on a regular basis.
- Monitor results and take action when targets are not met by the expected time.

Case Study

The CEO of PayRoll S.A. approved the investment required to form the PMO team and the implementation of the project management methodology from Cadence, including project management training and leadership training. He also provided clear direction on business objectives to be met. He held the team accountable for rapid implementation of the initiative and gave team members very aggressive deadlines for delivering the expected business results.

Quevedo, the PMO leader, and his project management team met daily to maintain operations, ensure customer satisfaction, and promote a culture of improvement. Quevedo started tracking project performance and business financial performance and very rapidly demonstrated the value proposition of his function to the organization. The company was able to see the results of its project management improvement effort.

- Project length significantly decreased.
- Customer satisfaction improved tremendously.
- Project profitability increased.

Lesson

Ongoing reviews of process performance are important to keep the organization focused on improving results. Business owners should continue to report metrics to identify the project, program, and portfolio processes that need further improvement to align to the organizational objectives.

Step 8: Re-Assess and Continue Improving

The design solution developed in step 4 proposes both continuous and disruptive change. The organization needs time to stabilize after the plan is implemented. Often, additional assessments are planned to benchmark the progress made toward objectives or organizational maturity. The metrics may even indicate that the initiative has failed in parts. So it may be necessary to launch another effort to propose further solutions and to plan and implement new initiatives.

Key Practices

A process of continuous assessments will give the organization an opportunity to continue to optimize performance. A reassessment can help you validate the team's perception of the effectiveness of the changes.

A governance body is useful to manage the processes and improvement efforts in your organization. This committee will help keep your processes updated. Your organization should use the same approach for continued improvement efforts that it took when initially implementing changes. As before, you should understand reasons for any changes and the purpose of the changes and develop a good implementation plan that can be effectively adopted and monitored.

Case Study

A year after the initial implementation, PayRoll S.A. requested a formal OPM3® ProductSuite assessment with a certified OPM3® assessor (myself) to validate its PMO processes and provide a baseline assessment of its maturity to help it continue to improve. The OPM3® assessor and consultant concluded that the organization now had a very high maturity level. Its improvement initiative had resulted in a dramatic increase in metrics and customer satisfaction.

The OPM3® assessor gave PMO leader Quevedo and his team a full list of new challenges and opportunities for improvement. They will continue the improvement process, and they expect to be assessed again next year and eventually reach the highest level of maturity to maximize business value.

Lesson

Continue to review project, program, and portfolio metrics to determine how well they are aligned with organizational needs and objectives. This process can be tailored or adapted to re-launching an assessment or initiating new improvement processes.

Final Thoughts

In this chapter, you learned how to apply a proven method to evaluate your organizational environment and identify your true challenges. We talked about looking at your organization from an end-to-end perspective. I shared an assessment approach and an improvement plan and described how involving the entire organization and including subject matter experts in the process improvement team can help you create the right solution. A good implementation plan is the key for change adoption, and the assessment process ends only when your performance level reaches the stated improvement objectives.

With this knowledge, you are ready to start down the path to rapidly transforming your business and delivering the business results you expect and need!

Key Steps to Improving the Project Environment

- Perform an initial evaluation of the problem to be solved and set expectations for the organization going forward, all focused on improving project implementation and employee and customer satisfaction.

- Design and implement a simple and repeatable project management methodology based on project management best practices and standard processes, with a parameter of what will be good enough to meet the specific needs of the client without taking time to include unnecessary processes, activities, or things that would just be nice to have.

- Create a PMO culture by designating clear roles and responsibilities and authority levels for everyone involved in the improvement effort, and emphasize team accountability for success and failure.

- Engage executives in the creation of the PM processes, and create an executive communication plan to present project tracking and results on a regular basis.

- Ensure that the PMO aligns with organizational objectives.

- Perform an organizational project management assessment, and implement improvement opportunities.

CHAPTER 9

OPM Practices: The Turnaround of Indian Railways

Pavan Kumar Gorakavi

Is your organization facing significant financial, social, or political challenges due to the changing business environment? Are your project results accessible to a large range of external stakeholders? If not, your organization should try organizational project management (OPM) practices to yield better results. In this chapter, we will consider different OPM practices and their benefits by looking at the classic example of the turnaround of Indian Railways.

Public scrutiny is a fundamental challenge for corporate leaders and senior project management professionals who are working on large, complex, or global projects. Success isn't usually guaranteed, and criticism is vocal and public. So we want to explore several essential components of a successful business transformation in the face of entrenched public opinion and rigid culture. In this chapter, you will find:

- A public-sector case study that is applicable to complex and risky projects
- A process for navigating through political and financial challenges
- Practical advice for communicating a message during a change process.

An Overview of Indian Railways

Indian Railways is the principal public transport system in India. It is one of the top five national railway systems in the world. Indian Railways is also one of the largest public-service organizations in India, with a capital investment of 550 billion rupees and 1.4 million employees. The total length of the railway is 63,465 kilometers (the second longest in the world). Nearly 7,000 railway stations serve more than 14 million passengers per day. Figure 9-1 gives a quick overview of other Indian Railways data.[1]

The Government of India's Ministry of Railways department manages Indian Railways. To facilitate the management of this gigantic organization, Indian Railways is decentralized into 16 zones (and a metro system in Kolkata). Each zone is headed by a general manager who reports directly to the railway board.[2]

In the late 1990s, Indian Railways' financials deteriorated because of social, economic, and political conditions. The Indian government's public policy considered railways a social sector. The operational impacts of this policy were:

• Imposed social obligations for providing employment

• 1.4 million employees
• More than 14 million passengers per day
• 63,465 kilometers of rail
• 37,119 passenger service vehicles
• 222,379 wagons
• 7,910 locomotives

Figure 9-1 Quick Data on Indian Railways

• Stated and unstated social requirements for affordable and subsidized transportation.

These public policy constraints created a perfect storm that, despite increasing revenue, drove the Indian Railways system into a financial crisis that was evident in the sharp decline in dividend payouts between 2000 and 2001 (Figure 9-2). The search for a way to turn Indian Railways' dismal outlook around led to organizational project management.[3]

	1996	1997	1998	1999	2000	2001
Operating ratio	82.45	86.22	90.92	93.34	93.31	98.30
Dividend payments (Rs crores)	1,264	1,507	1,489	1,742	1,890	308
Passenger revenue (Rs crores)	6,113	6,616	7,554	8,527	9,556	10,483
Freight revenue (Rs crores)	15,290	16,668	19,866	19,960	22,341	23,305
Employees (millions)	1.587	1.584	1.579	1.578	1.577	1.545
Total wages (Rs crores)	9,363	10,514	14,141	15,611	16,289	18,841

(1 crore rupee = 10 million rupees (Rs))
(1 USD = around 45 Rs)

Figure 9-2 Key Financial Indicators for Indian Railways, 1996–2001

An organization with such a huge employee base also has considerable social responsibilities and contributes significantly to the country's GDP. With size come more challenges. In the late 1990s, Indian Railways' social challenges included:

- Increases in wage rates
- Massive organizational structure
- Employee unions
- Subsidies.

As part of its social obligations, Indian Railways carries many commodities below cost, provides social uplifts, subsidized its tariffs, and operates uneconomical branch lines.

The environmental challenges the organization faced in the late 1990s included:

- Economic, social, and political situations
- Competitive market; other transportation alternatives
- Accelerating pace of technology change
- Legislative changes (similar to Sarbanes-Oxley Act, banking/financial reporting).

Applying Organizational Project Management to Indian Railways

Many types of organizations can improve business results by implementing a process that links strategy to projects. Organizational project management provides systematic management of project, program, and portfolio work to smoothly transform messy, conflicting, yet essential requirements into deliverables that drive efficiency by improving processes, practices, or capabilities. OPM practices facilitate strong linkage between planning, execution, and evaluation. This linkage helps organizations manage projects in a predictable, directional, and reliable manner. Is OPM itself predictable? No. A good OPM practice therefore includes proactive planning and flexible reactive approaches.

In this chapter, we will discuss how Indian Railways implemented OPM practices to overcome its financial crisis. Though Indian Railways probably did not realize that it was implementing OPM, the organization nevertheless implemented a commonsense turnaround that we can see contained significant features of OPM. Figure 9-3 illustrates the basic features of the OPM life cycle, including the following four-step process:

1. Assess the initial problem.
2. Analyze the value of a proposed program.
3. Implement a strategy.
4. Evaluate the outcome.

Let's follow the story of Indian Railways' turnaround according to our proposed OPM four-step process.

Step 1: Assess the Initial Problem

Because Indian Railways plays a vital role in India's social, political, and economic livelihood, the Indian government recognized the significance of Indian Railways' financial crisis. The government appointed an independent committee led by Rakesh Mohan to analyze Indian Railways' operations.[4] The committee found that the following situations led to the organization's financial crisis:

- Poor productivity
- Rising employee wages
- Declining government budgetary support
- Bad investments in unproductive projects
- Subsidized prices for lower-class passengers

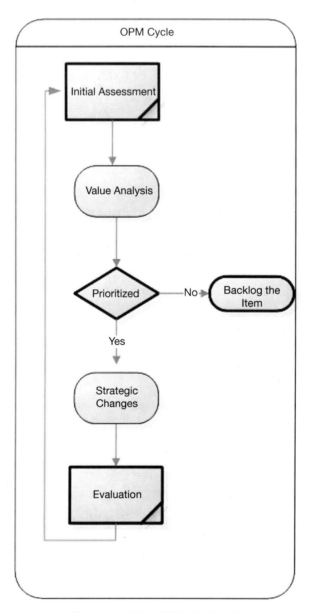

Figure 9-3 The OPM Life Cycle

- Overpricing freight and fares for higher-class passengers, leading to loss of market share
- An increasingly open economy, which created a more competitive transportation system.

The Rakesh Mohan committee found that urgent action was needed to revitalize the organization so that it could continue to serve the nation. It recommended significant short-term and long-term changes for repositioning Indian Railways:

- Raising freight fares
- Upgrading rolling stock
- Increasing the speed of freight trains
- Improving signaling technology
- Increasing container terminal yields
- Instituting a tariff to rebalance fares paid by upper-class and lower-class passengers.

The committee also suggested the following cost-reduction and revenue-generating initiatives to stabilize Indian Railways' financial health:

- Asset sales
- A reduction of at least 20 percent of the workforce
- The government should reimburse Indian Railways for any subsidized programs.

OPM Key Practices

The assessment life cycle should include an initial assessment of the organization's problem(s), risks, and key issues. Management can prioritize the initiatives based upon the most pressing social, political, economic, and technological challenges. Iterative assessments yield a better analysis.

Is This Applicable to Your Organization?

Does your organization need to assess its problems? Would an assessment spur organizational changes?

Step 2: Analyze the Value of a Proposed Program

Indian Railways management realized that there was a need to change the organization's vision. Former railway minister Nitish Kumar explicitly stated in his 2001–2002 budget speech that Indian Railways projects had to have a greater customer focus and market orientation. In accordance with this new mandate, Indian Railways:

- Analyzed projects based on value
- Implemented cost-reduction strategies
- Reorganized the organization
- Implemented decentralization
- Implemented technology to
  ○ Improve revenue transparency
  ○ Support supply chain improvements.

As a result of these efforts, the operating ratio, which was as high as 98.3 in 2001, fell to 83.2 in 2007. There was a significant reduction in the number of employees, from 1.545 million in 2001 to 1.412 million in 2006. There was not an official layoff; instead, the Railways ministry did not fill all the positions vacated when employees retired. Higher efficiency, new technological advances, new strategies, value-based project analysis, and dynamic leadership all helped make Indian Railways one of the top revenue-generating public service organizations in India.

The growing Indian economy—the GDP rose more than seven percent between 2001 and 2006—also helped Indian Railways generate more revenue from both freight and passengers.[5] Key financial indicators for 2001–2006 are shown in Figure 9-4.

OPM Key Practices

Project portfolio management—similar to Indian Railways' program value analysis—is used by many organizations to align project work with corporate strategy. See Chapters 2 and 3 for detailed discussions of portfolio management.

Is This Applicable to Your Organization?

Many initiatives are forged without consideration of value. In the United States, one of the federal government's current priorities is health care

	2001	2002	2003	2004	2005	2006
Operating ratio	98.3	96.02	92.3	92.1	91	83.2
Dividend payments (Rs crores)	308	1,337	2,715	3,087	3,199	3,287
Passenger revenue (Rs crores)	10,483	11,196	12,575	13,298	14,113	15,126
Freight revenue (Rs crores)	23,305	24,845	26,505	27,618	30,778	36,287
Employees (millions)	1.545	1.511	1.472	1.442	1.424	1.412
Total wages (Rs crores)	18,841	19,214	19,915	20,929	22,553	23,954

(1 crore rupee = 10 million rupees (Rs))
(1 USD = around 45 Rs)

Figure 9-4 Key Financial Indicators for Indian Railways, 2001–06

reform. However, the value in relation to the cost is not fully understood and remains controversial. Value analysis needs to be performed for organizational initiatives. Is your organization's corporate vision disconnected from a realistic assessment of the value of its programs?

Step 3: Implement a Strategy

In five years, an unwieldy organization with 1.4 million employees and significant public-service obligations turned its financial position around from not being able to pay dividends to being solidly profitable. This financial turnaround can be credited to five factors: effective leadership, value-based analysis, technological upgrades, strategic structural changes, and capitalized opportunities in the social and economic environment.

Effective Leadership

Former railway minister Nitish Kumar demonstrated strong vision and solid project selection and political skills between 2001 and 2004, as did Lalu Prasad Yadav in 2005–2009, and as Mamta Banerjee is doing as current railway minister.

Value-Based Analysis

Indian Railways' value-based analysis of projects and different modules of business helped the organization make decisions about outsourcing, divestiture, and discontinuance. Specifically, Indian Railways decided to privatize lease and parcel services.

Technological Upgrades

Upgrading technology was a priority, both to support other initiatives and to reduce corruption through revenue transparency. In his 2006 budget speech, former railway minister Lalu Prasad Yadav said, "The technological upgrades in every field of Railway working will be given the utmost priority so that the reliability of services can be improved to gain customers' confidence and also bring down the operating and maintenance costs."[6] The investment did improve reliability, reduce operating costs, and increase process efficiency, and it ultimately increased customer confidence.

Having realized the significance of technological upgrades in reducing operating costs and gaining market share, Indian Railways has prioritized projects for developing high-capacity wagons, 25-ton axle-load wagons, advanced signaling and telecommunication technology, and wider use of information technology. The organization has developed many new applications:

- New ticketing and passenger service applications
- Freight service applications
- Finance applications
- MIS applications for assets management.[7]

Indian Railways developed a freight operating information system to improve freight logistics support. Because freight revenue has contributed to more than 60 percent of the total revenue of Indian Railways, heavy expectations were placed on this system. The system was successfully developed, and it made a remarkable improvement in the operating efficiency of freight transportation. According to Lalu Prasad Yadav,

> There has been a remarkable improvement in operating efficiency of freight transportation with the help of Freight Operating Information System. In the first phase of this project, Rake Management System has been implemented at all major locations. In the second phase, Terminal Management System will also be implemented at all major locations. Apart from this, work is also progressing speedily on control charting, crew management, and Coaching Operations Information System. Next year, all efforts will be made to implement Control Charting System on all the divisions. The complete computerization of Control Office, Coaching Operations Information System, and interfacing of both these systems with National Train Enquiry System will directly benefit passengers and other rail users.[8]

Strategic Structural Changes

Indian Railways' management made some structural changes and some cost-effective productive changes and changed their vision. These changes helped significantly in boosting Indian Railways' profitability. Specifically, Indian Railways:

- Reduced costs by reducing the labor force.
- Further decentralized the organization by increasing the number of zones from 9 to 16.

- Offered cash incentives to freight customers to reduce freight turnaround time. In other words, because incentives were offered to freight customers to free up the wagons faster, handling capacity increased.

- Changed the vision and focus of Indian Railways to address the competitive market and serve customers better.

- Developed a competitive tariff, computerized ticketing, and several other customer service programs and increased passenger comforts.

- Implemented additional safety programs like advance communication systems, additional railway police, and warning systems.[9]

Freight accounts for most of Indian Railways' revenue. Thus, the organization instituted a competitive freight tariff, increased axle load, and improved wagon turnaround time. This improved Indian Railways' positioning relative to other road and air transportation options.

Capitalized Opportunities in the Social and Economic Environment

The Indian economy grew between 2004 and 2007 (Figure 9-5). Economic growth and stable political conditions had a positive impact on Indian Railways' freight and passenger services; the organization took good advantage of this growing economy and stable political situation to reposition itself as a highly profitable organization.

Year	2001	2002	2003	2004	2005	2006	2007
GDP	4.4	5.2	3.8	8.5	7.5	9	9.2

Figure 9-5 India's GDP[10]

The financial crisis that began in 2007 affected most of the industries throughout the world. Despite the financial crisis, Indian Railways' freight cargo grew 5 percent, and traffic receipts increased by 11.4 percent during 2008–2009.[11]

Step 4: Evaluate the Outcome

Indian Railways has its own budget sessions, attended by government dignitaries, politicians, and other individuals responsible for social welfare, during which various projects, financial statements, financial budget allocations, subsidies, committee specifications, and organizational results are evaluated.

OPM Key Practices

Analysis, implementation, and evaluation of organizational improvement initiatives are iterative. Change is inevitable, and the process needs to reflect these cycles.

Is This Applicable to Your Organization?

OPM is about identifying the problem, adopting a strategy, implementing that strategy, validating the results—and adapting to change over time. How is your organization adapting?

Final Thoughts

Organizations can proactively facilitate successful projects by performing high-level initial assessments and risk analyses, prioritizing tasks through value analyses, managing changes carefully, and evaluating results in an iterative and incremental manner. Though all projects are unique, these basic OPM practices may help drive your project toward its optimal destination.

Notes

1   World Bank Railways Database, http://siteresources.worldbank.org/INTRAILWAYS/Resources/514687-1185223803413/RDB_June_8_2007.XLS (accessed February 1, 2010). For more information about the World Bank's Railway Database, see Louis S. Thompson and Julie M. Fraser, "World Bank's Railway Database," Transport No. RW-6 (The World Bank, Transportation, Water, and Urban Development Department, October 1993). Available online at http://siteresources.worldbank.org/INTTRANSPORT/Resources/336291-1119275973157/td-rw6.pdf (accessed March 9, 2010).

2 Indian Railway Zones, http://www.indianrail.gov.in/ir_zones.pdf (accessed February 1, 2010).

3 Desh Gupta and Milind Sathye, "Financial turnaround of the Indian Railways: Good Luck or Good Management," ASARC Working Paper 2008/06. Available online at http://www.scribd.com/doc/3509828/ Financial-turnaround-of-the-Indian-Railways (accessed February 1, 2010); World Bank Railways Database, http://siteresources.worldbank.org/ INTRAILWAYS/Resources/514687-1185223803413/RDB_June_8_2007. XLS (accessed February 1, 2010).

4 Indian Railways Accounts Service, "Rakesh Mohan Committee Report— Highlights of the Executive Summary." Available online at http://www. irastimes.org/rkmreporthighexsummary.htm (accessed February 1, 2010)

5 Desh Gupta and Milind Sathye, "Financial turnaround of the Indian Railways: Good Luck or Good Management," ASARC Working Paper 2008/06. Available online at http://www.scribd.com/doc/3509828/ Financial-turnaround-of-the-Indian-Railways (accessed February 1, 2010); World Bank Railways Database, http://siteresources.worldbank.org/ INTRAILWAYS/Resources/514687-1185223803413/RDB_June_8_2007. XLS (accessed February 1, 2010).

6 Shri. Lalu Prasad Yadav, "Speech of Shri Lalu Prasad Introducing the Railway Budget 2006-07," February 24, 2006. Available online at http://www.indianrail.gov.in/Railwayshtml.htm (accessed February 1, 2010).

7 Ministry of Railways (Railway Board), "Information Technology Security Policy for Indian Railways: Report of the Inter-Disciplinary Core Group," August 2007. Available online at http://www.indianrailways.gov.in/deptts/ cis/IT-circulars/RecomSecPol.pdf (accessed February 1, 2010).

8 Shri. Lalu Prasad Yadav, "Speech of Shri. Lalu Prasad Introducing the Railway Budget 2006-07," February 24, 2006. Available online at http://www.indianrail.gov.in/Railwayshtml.htm (accessed February 1, 2010).

9 Desh Gupta and Milind Sathye, "Financial turnaround of the Indian Railways: Good Luck or Good Management." Available online at http://www.scribd.com/doc/3509828/Financial-turnaround-of-the-Indian-Railways (accessed February 1, 2010).

10 Desh Gupta and Milind Sathye, "Financial turnaround of the Indian Railways: Good Luck or Good Management." Available online at http://www.scribd.com/doc/3509828/Financial-turnaround-of-the-Indian-Railways (accessed February 1, 2010).

11 *Speech of Kumari Mamata Banerjee Introducing the Railway Budget 2009–2010* (July 3, 2009). Available online at http://www.indianrail.gov. in/Speech_English_2009-10.pdf (accessed March 9, 2010).

CHAPTER 10

Sustainable Success: Leaders Who Transform

Marcia Daszko

The foundation of sustainable success in any organization is leadership and rapid organizational learning. The success of any strategic or project management initiative depends on effective, courageous leadership. A vice president for clinical development who is responsible for project management at a global pharmaceutical firm, Dr. Debra Vallner, stated, "Project managers may execute well, but the success of the organization is essentially based on how effective leadership is."

What is the role of leadership? How can a leader ensure that projects are optimally delivered to meet the business needs of the organization and serve customers? What philosophy of leadership do leaders need today and in the future to achieve a competitive edge? What leadership thinking and strategies accelerate progress and success, and what thinking or strategies lead to organizations' demise? This chapter will address those questions and deepen your understanding of organizational and project management success.

You will discover that the foundation for success of any strategic or project management initiative is leadership's commitment and ability to rapidly learn and adapt. In addition, you will discover:

- How leaders can think and lead differently to optimize the enterprise (a system) and ensure that major projects interdependently work toward the success of the organization
- That a leader's knowledge and effectiveness defines whether the organization and its projects can be managed and succeed
- How an organizational strategic compass (OSC), a tool that is too infrequently used in strategic and operational efforts, can help leaders set direction toward the effective management and implementation of projects.

Unfortunately, organizations rarely engage in systems thinking, the kind of thinking so desperately needed for sustainable success. Executives and managers try to maximize rather than optimize, but optimization is the difference between long-term success and failure.

Defining Leadership

Many organizations have too many projects, too few resources, internal competition for rewards, too little focus, and most critically, little understanding about how all the parts of the organization need to work *together*. Projects are the work that supports the direction a company is going in and helps accomplish the strategic goals and compelling purpose of the organization. But without a clear purpose and a methodology to accomplish it together, it doesn't matter how great the projects and people are, how hard the people work, how efficient the processes are, what "best efforts" and "best practices" are used, or how many defects Six Sigma analysis—a well-known application for statistical process control—reveals.

Leadership must create a system and optimize it. If not, the parts of the organization can all be great, yet the system (the organization itself) can easily fail.

A *system* is a network of functions or activities (processes) within an organization that work together toward the aim of the organization. How the parts *interact*—not how the parts *act*, separately or independently—is critical.

Leadership is not easy. It requires an ability to inspire people and to communicate effectively to engage them and harness their commitment to a purpose larger than themselves. It requires executives to have a new way of thinking, knowledge, and traits that are often uncommon in today's workplace, including:

- The courage to challenge bad practices like short-term, bottom-line thinking or slow, fear-based decision-making
- The knowledge to base decisions on data observed over time and in context
- The patience and commitment to focus on innovating, to sustain the long-term health of an organization
- The compassion needed to create jobs instead of cutting costs through layoffs, grabbing the annual bonus, and abandoning the company.

Leadership requires knowledge that challenges what is currently being taught in many of the "best" universities by the "best" professors churning out the "best" job candidates with the highest GPAs.

In reality, if we buy into the "best" mentality, our achievements will fall short and we will create win-lose strategies in work and life. Why do the "best" job candidates, "best" schools, "best" efforts, and "best" practices often lead our organizations, our projects, and our cultures into decline and dysfunction? Lack of leadership, simply and fundamentally. We need leadership with systems knowledge that is rarely understood and practiced today. Without this knowledge, executives and managers manage individual departments, silos, and divisions without understanding that the whole is larger than the sum of many parts.

Let's think about a car. If we take the "best" parts from the Volvo, Mercedes, Lexus, Mini Cooper, and BMW and put them together, will we have a car that works? Of course not. This is why many organizations and projects fail. We think that if we bring the "best" candidates from the "best" schools and use the "best" practices, we have the recipe for success. Instead, we have a sure recipe for failure.

The systems and statistical knowledge needed in organizations is rarely taught in our schools and universities. But if the knowledge that is needed for organizational success was common, we would have people working collaboratively, doing good work (any work with committed people working together with a common aim and supportive resources), a strong and healthy worldwide economy, health care and education systems that serve people well, and a vibrant, sustainable environment.

Challenging the Status Quo

It is time to challenge our current leadership thinking. In a commencement address I recently gave to a group of naval intelligence officers who had just completed an intense two-week leadership class, I said, "Much of what I will share with you in the next 40 minutes will be in direct conflict with what you have just been taught; my aim is to provoke your thinking so that you will not adopt this status-quo learning or the practices that are commonly being used in corporate America, but have no common sense."

During my address, they began to think differently, to question, converse about, and challenge the idea of unquestioningly accepting current ways of thinking and leading. The status quo is based on too many managers being complacent or acting on autopilot. These behaviors don't challenge managers to question their current beliefs and assumptions; rather, they lead to poor decisions and outcomes and very dissatisfied customers.

The Essential Qualities of a Leader

So what exactly are we missing? Leadership requires:

- Knowledge, based in a theoretical foundation of management
- Systems and statistical thinking
- Knowledge about people and how they learn, interact, and are motivated
- The understanding that management is prediction; data are presented over time and in context for better decision-making
- A genuine commitment to rigorous and continual learning, especially at the executive level
- Patience with chaos and upheaval and the ability to facilitate solutions and manage the chaos and upheaval
- Dedication to articulating the organization's direction well and repeatedly
- Listening deeply, with perseverance and tenacity
- Respect, understanding, and care for people
- Courage and humility.

Leaders with these qualities can discern the difference between management fads and powerful transformation and can identify supporting projects and tools that can accelerate their organizations' progress. So how are you doing? Are you a leader? What is the legacy you will leave? What will your employees and customers say about your leadership and the ease of doing business with your organization?

Among other things, leaders must transform their organizations; help build a solid organizational foundation; and engage the customer to understand what the customer really needs, today and in the future.

Leaders Transform

Focused leaders work tirelessly to transform their organizations. They are adept at devising strategies to continually improve, innovate, focus on delivering quality, and commit to adding value and serving customers. They create leadership and communications as systems that everyone must work to continually improve. Leaders build and guide a portfolio of interdependent projects and operations that lead to system optimization and a culture that delivers continual learning (the only hope for a competitive edge), progress, and success. They ask, "What? What if? How?" They never accept the status quo. They never fall into complacency, arrogance, or greed. They strive to be responsive. They identify fear in the organization and work relentlessly to reduce it and build trust.

"Old thinking" in organizations often means relying on business and management models that fundamentally don't work. We know they don't work. They create silos, finger-pointing, blame, cultures full of fear, and analysis paralysis, and they lead to poor decision-making and results.

Leaders Build

Project portfolio management and product development succeed when an organization has built a foundation with a clear purpose and strategies, optimized systems and processes, and a culture of collaboration. Leadership creates the strategies and operational planning, defines key business issues, and forms project and process improvement teams to do the work that will deliver the business needs and serve customers.

What happens when the organization, including the project managers and teams, do not understand the purpose they are trying to achieve together? Projects drag on and are late and over budget; employees become tired and frustrated; management panics and forces out "something" that doesn't meet customers' needs. The business suffers from higher costs, greater inefficiencies, and poor quality and is sent into a spiraling decline.

Leaders Engage the Customer

A Fortune 500 company recently lost a major contract with a client it had had for more than 25 years. Project teams had diligently used project management metrics to track progress, but the company was lacking engaged leaders who understood what the customer needed today and in the future. Even though the project metrics reflected the specific characteristics of the project, they didn't support the strategic goals of the company. You can't substitute metrics-tracking for leadership.

A project group can, for example, track the number of technical manuals and documents it writes and the percentage of projects completed on time, but these metrics don't tell us if the team is writing the content the customer needs or writing it in a way the customer can easily use. What's more valuable: tracking the schedule or spending time visiting the customer to understand how they use the product and what they will need in the future? (Keep in mind that it is our job to innovate, not the customer's.) Leadership must create a system that links project work to supporting and serving customers.

The Organizational Strategic Compass

Organizations are more successful if their leaders understand that their role is strategic and synthetic, not analytical. They should ask, "How do all the elements of the business weave together?", not "How do we break the whole into parts—and then try to understand or micromanage the parts?" This kind of analytical thinking is the most common kind of dysfunctional leadership thinking today and is the cause for the rapid failure of American businesses.

An organizational strategic compass (OSC) is a model that guides leadership thinking and helps leaders develop a cohesive business strategy (Figure 10-1). Leaders don't use road maps, which are useful only when you know you are going straight from point A to point B. Rather, leaders use a compass to guide their journey into new and unknown territory, the future. The OSC can help leaders determine where they want to go. It encourages them to look closely at the terrain, the barriers, and the

Organizational Strategic Compass (OSC)
The five parts of the OSC must work interdependently together.

PURPOSE and DIRECTION

- In what direction are we going, and why?

- How do we create an organization in which everyone can contribute to this direction?

PRINCIPLES

- What principles and behaviors do we want to exhibit?

STRATEGIES

- How will we get where we're heading?

CUSTOMERS

- To whom will we deliver our strategies?

SUCCESS METRICS

- How will we measure success?

Figure 10-1 Organizational Strategic Compass

opportunities (markets and potential markets) and make necessary shifts in response. Guided by this compass, leaders can adjust, adapt, and be agile, responsive, and flexible in serving their customers.

An OSC has five foundational and interdependent parts. Using an OSC is essential for management teams, and it is often helpful for project teams, though project teams may also use road maps, process maps, and other tools.

Strategic thinking means asking more questions and deeply involving everyone in a challenging learning process. When you use an OSC, brainstorming hundreds of ideas is replaced with a more important activity, brainstorming the *questions* that must be asked and answered. (Isn't that a novel idea—and a departure from many managers' obsession with brainstorming ideas for quick fixes?)

An OSC replaces the traditional and often static strategic planning process that includes setting strategies, objectives, targets, and numerical goals; doing a strengths, weaknesses, opportunities, and threats analysis (SWOT analysis); defining individual competencies; and creating dashboards. An OSC guides leaders to a higher level of thinking.

The OSC comprises five parts:

1. *Purpose and direction:* Where are we going and why?

2. *Strategies:* How will we get where we're heading?

3. *Principles:* What do we stand for, and what behaviors illustrate our principles?

4. *Customers:* To whom will we deliver our strategies?

5. *Success metrics:* How will we measure success?

All five parts are interdependent and must work together for success.

As they say at the circus, "Don't try this at home"—or, in this case, don't complete the OSC alone. Make sure to work with a facilitator who has transformation and systems knowledge. In addition to providing vital expertise, the facilitator has another essential role: to ask questions from an outside perspective and to challenge your thinking so you experience profound ah-ha moments and do not fall into groupthink.

The point of the OSC is to achieve different—better—results based on new insights. Too often groups are so busy patting themselves on the back for their successes that they don't focus on strategy for the future and don't see the grenade that a competitor is tossing at them, often a competitor they either didn't see coming or did not take seriously.

Project Management and the Organizational Strategic Compass

Strategic leadership and project management are linked when leadership develops and communicates the OSC to the organization, the major subsystems and processes of the organization have been identified, and project teams are formed to work interactively to support the optimization and aim of the enterprise. Continual communication, guidance, and feedback will allow the cooperation and information-sharing necessary for progress and success. Ongoing improvement processes will accelerate learning, and the rapid acquisition of knowledge will expedite the enterprise's race toward a competitive advantage.

The Management Principles of W. Edwards Deming

Organizations are facing pressure to compete like never before, and many leaders are confronting new challenges. Leaders who can draw upon a foundation of management principles that promote system optimization can adapt, respond, survive, grow, succeed, and create a new future. Most leaders do not have this knowledge or much experience.

The management principles that W. Edwards Deming introduced in Japan to help businesses recover after World War II are still not well-known and are rarely implemented. Auto industry executives adopted these leadership principles in the 1980s to renew the American auto industry, but they were abandoned when the focus of the auto industry and then big business in general became the bottom line and stock prices, rather than the health of a sustainable enterprise. Focusing on the bottom line destroys organizations.[1]

Deming's principles offer organizations anywhere in the world the strategic and operational foundation to transform themselves and the focus necessary to compete in our global economy. Though they were developed decades ago, these principles foreshadowed the evolution of business models and strategies that are important today: the relentless integration of customer feedback into creating a more effective, innovative system; the evolution of the modern, information-based supply chain; and collaborative, interdependent connectivity within organizations that demands people work, learn, improve, and innovate *together.*[2]

Deming's writings on teamwork, collaboration, rigorous training, and working closely with suppliers were among his most controversial and groundbreaking. He emphatically stated that the customer is the most important part of the production line, that fear inhibits cooperation and leads to the creation of false data, and that management by objectives (especially numerical goals and targets) creates organizational misalignment.[3]

When leaders truly understand these principles, among others, there is a huge opportunity for them, along with project managers and employees, to make profound changes happen. Leaders using leadership theories based on systems thinking have fundamental insight into the changes in structure and strategy that organizations must make as they pursue the strategic imperatives of innovation, speed, flexibility, quality, and creating value for customers and future markets.

Deming asserted that the greatest leverage for unleashing the potential for human performance in organizations (and project teams), and thus for improving organizational performance, lies in rethinking the way we construct organizational reality.[4] Many of the barriers to quality, improvement, and innovation are of our own making. Letting go of the assumptions that underlie prevailing business models is the key to removing artificially created obstacles to improvement and innovation. This approach raises organizational performance to new levels. We can, for example, improve and improve the buggy whip, but that improvement will never get us to a horseless carriage, an automobile, or a hybrid car.

Most business models that fail do not appreciate the degree of connectedness between elements of the organizations: between department silos, between customer-supplier relationships, between organizations and their customers, between the flow of process improvement and project teams, and between measurement systems and behavior. In too many organizations, there is a disconnect between the direction the leadership team is taking the organization and the project teams' work. Each project team or department works alone without understanding the aim of the larger whole or how the team or department fits into and contributes to it. Often, teams are unaware of the project work being done by other teams. Leadership does not guide the optimization of all the work or link it to the value it offers customers.

Individuals and project teams can work hard and make their best effort, but the enterprise may still fail. Leadership is responsible for creating the system and optimizing it so that everyone is working *together* toward a common aim. Project teams can work interdependently toward that aim and the strategic goals of the organization.

Leadership and Systems Thinking

Executives must lead and optimize the entire enterprise. All the parts (e.g., people, materials, projects, resources, operations, branding, ideas) must work well together. Unfortunately, many management models and tools are really just parts of a tool kit, and the parts don't work together. How can executives, managers, and employees effectively measure progress and success? How can project teams learn how their work contributes to a larger whole? This section will help leaders answer these critical questions.

In 1987, Deming articulated a "system of profound knowledge" comprising four interdependent elements, including appreciation for a system, knowledge about variation, theory of knowledge, and psychology.[5] Here, Deming's concepts are expanded upon to include systems thinking and system optimization; understanding variation; theory of knowledge; theory of people, learning styles, and motivation. Figure 10-2 shows how these elements interrelate, and the following section describes each of the elements in detail.

- *Systems thinking and system optimization.* A *system* is a network of interdependent components that work together to serve its purpose. Systems thinking must be applied for projects *and* for organizations

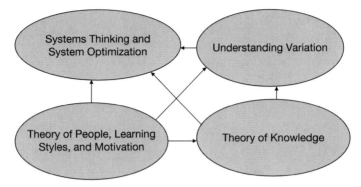

Figure 10-2 A Systemic Approach for Applying Leadership to Organizations and Project Management

to succeed because project and organizational success depend on each other. Overemphasizing certain parts of the system breaks it down. A common example: dividing companies into departments without understanding their interdependencies or how the work flows.

Another example comes from Brenda Wright, Director of Technical Training for a Fortune 500 storage company:

> System optimization doesn't always refer to automation or computers either. We had a challenge to break down cross-organizational barriers and define a simplified workflow. Many teams wanted a one-click solution, yet each team had their preferred approach. Using the OSC model, they shared their perspectives and then created a unified system that worked and flowed well for the entire organization.

- *Understanding variation.* Variation comes from many sources: the environment, subsystems, processes, resources, and culture. Too often, managers tamper with systems that are in control, making things worse. Or they blame individuals for problems that are actually attributable to the other five sources. It is the system that delivers the outcomes—and only management is responsible for the system. Common-cause variation is normal, and people are only a small part of that equation. It is crucial for leaders to understand theory of variation and statistical thinking; otherwise, they react, make poor decisions, and create chaos and more waste and inefficiency.

- *Theory of knowledge.* Deming wrote that the theory of knowledge (TOK) "helps us to understand that management in any form is prediction."[6] We need a theory, a plan, a prediction to manage and to learn. Even simple events require a plan. For example, when we plan to go to a baseball game, we make assumptions about transportation and weather; we predict how our plan will go; and we discover whether our assumptions, plans, and predictions work out in the end. Based on our experience, we adjust our assumptions, plans, and predictions in the future. It's the same in business: Measuring our progress and achievements helps us determine whether we are going in the right direction to accomplish our organization's strategic purpose, but we must be careful not to get caught up in measurement mania—trying to measure things that can't be quantified.

- *Theory of People, Learning Styles, and Motivation.* Psychology helps us to understand group dynamics, different learning styles, human interaction and behavior, and intrinsic and extrinsic motivation, as well as fear, trust, communication, resistance to change, individual and organizational learning, and barriers to improvement.

This framework illustrates the leadership thinking and foundation that are necessary for effective, successful project management. Each of the four elements is detailed below.

Systems Thinking and System Optimization

Leaders must understand how systems work. The role of each part of a system is to contribute to optimizing the whole system. It is not to maximize itself. It is to create cooperation, not internal competition. Think of an orchestra, a human body, a car—how well would they work if their parts were competing with each other? Would the orchestra play noise or music? Would the body function well or go into shock? Would the car go down the road or sputter and stop? The greater the interdependence between parts, the greater the need for cooperation between them. It is the job of leadership to make sure the parts work together—and this job cannot be delegated!

When a leadership team develops an organizational strategic compass (OSC) and defines where the enterprise is going and some ideas for how it will get there, it begins to define its major issues and opportunities. It can then determine which projects must receive focus and resources. The success of the organization depends on how those key issues, projects, and processes are managed interdependently so that they all work toward the success of the whole organization (Figure 10-3).

In *The Fifth Discipline: The Art & Practice of the Learning Organization*, author Peter Senge describes the automobile industry's awakening to systems thinking.[7] When American automobile manufacturers began to take Japanese competition seriously, they dissected engines from their cars and

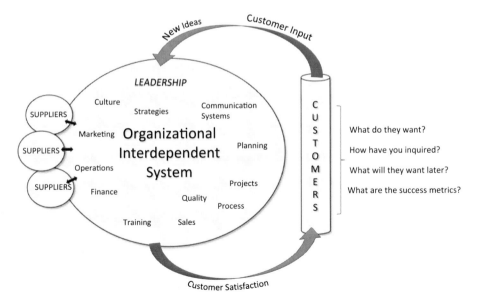

Figure 10-3 System Diagram

from Japanese cars. They found that three subassemblies in the American car engine used three differently sized bolts. This necessitated three sets of tools, three sets of inventory, and so on. The Japanese car used the same-sized bolt throughout. The conclusion was that each American subassembly was intended to be independently effective. In the Japanese production system, someone was responsible for making sure that the entire assembly was *interdependently* effective.[8]

All parts of an enterprise are connected: systems, subsystems, processes, projects, materials, resources, people, teams, products, and services. All contribute. But when the *system* doesn't deliver the results we want or need, what do we do? We blame people. However, only leadership is accountable for the success of systems because leaders create the systems. Individuals are responsible for contributing their part, but cannot be held accountable for a system they did not create or its outcomes, contrary to common practice in America and other countries that have adopted Western-style management.

It is important to remember that the optimization of a system does not necessarily result from the optimization of individual pieces. For example, Marian Hirsch, a senior technical editor at a global bioscience company, had an opportunity to help her team save a project and optimize the system. She explained:

> Last week I was in a department meeting to kick off a project that was a small part of introducing an updated version of a product (Product A). This introduction has important strategic implications for our business sector. We have a modernized format for manuals, and we are revising older ones to match this new format as products change.
>
> The writer assigned to this new project was assigned to update the format of a manual for a different product (Product B), the content of which wasn't scheduled to change for awhile. The manager wanted to slap some minor changes in the manual for Product A. I introduced the group to the system and its interactions: the product life cycle,

company strategy, impact on customers, etc. Together we discovered and learned that it was a better investment to completely update the manual for Product A; [the quality] would be better for customers, [and it would] have a longer life and make more sense for the investment of time and money. We could do the manual for Product B a few months down the road with no negative consequences. We just needed to look outside of our project as a team, look at the entire portfolio and marketing strategy, and understand how we fit in and were contributing toward it.

If top management focuses on creating systems in which people can collaborate on projects, continually improve processes, and innovate, then transformation is possible. If a company works on transformation and strives to make a difference internally and in society, won't financial success be a natural result?

Understanding Variation

Variation is normal. Numbers go up. Numbers go down. The trick is knowing how to manage variation (not just reduce it) and knowing when to act. Knowing when to take action and when to be hands-off is important for the successful implementation of project work. Otherwise, things that aren't broken get "fixed" (tampered with), and things that are broken are left unattended.

Six Sigma is a well-known application for statistical process control. Organizations using it attempt to improve processes so that there are only 3.4 defects or mistakes per million. However, many managers do not really understand what Six Sigma is or how to use it. They have rolled many dysfunctional practices into it, actually sub-optimizing their organizations in the process. The focus has been on defect detection rather than on quality process improvement, innovation, and system optimization.

Six Sigma has become one of the decade's most popular management fads, replacing sound management thinking. Six Sigma is only a tool, one that is often improperly used because many users do not understand statistical thinking or the theory of variation.

Understanding variation is key to reading any measurement of a process and, in turn, understanding how to optimize the enterprise. If data are interpreted improperly, managers will be very likely to react inappropriately and make poor decisions.

For example, Figure 10-4 shows a graph of data from the human resource department for a major client. The graph shows statistics for the amount of time the department takes to fill a critical hiring requisition. The data are useful to the company because they suggest uncontrolled conditions and show the average time it will take to fill hiring requisitions.

If managers analyze the data by comparing a single point in one year over a single point in another year, it can lead to over-adjustments. For example, comparing statistics from November 2007 against those from

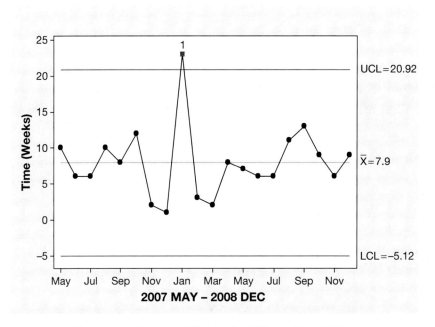

Figure 10-4 Time to Fill a Critical Hiring Requisition

November 2008 shows that the hiring time for that month was longer in 2008 than in 2007. While this is true, managers shouldn't extrapolate that minor variance to mean a significant, negative trend in hiring practices is occurring. Natural variances occur in any system; managers should look for long-term trends when deciding whether process-improvement initiatives are needed. The data point for January 2008, however, shows a clear outlier. Management should investigate what caused this divergence from the other data and ensure that control mechanisms are in place to prevent it from happening again.

As statistician and project logistics manager Diana Hagerty explained,

> Most management has no clue about variation. Project managers are forced to work with poorly designed tools and standard operating procedures that make things worse. Project management software cannot even deal with common-cause variation. It's useful for tracking progress, but completely useless for making predictions. Garbage in, garbage out—and people rely on it without asking any questions, much less pertinent ones! It doesn't tell you if the process is stable. One example is when one of my technical leads tried to trim our team's schedule to fit a more aggressive product launch—the software added six weeks to the project!

Theory of Knowledge

People managing systems and working in them need to work together to develop methods by which processes can be continually improved and results achieved. The most critical question for improvement is, "What are we trying to accomplish together?" (The question "What are we trying to accomplish?" is not sufficient; adding the word "together" encourages people to look at a larger aim, not just their own part in it.) The next question should be, "By what method?" In other words, what will the process be? Finally, we must ask, "What measures of improvement will we use so that we can identify change and know if it is significant?"

Company leaders cannot merely set numerical goals, objectives, and targets without also simultaneously discussing the plan and methods by which progress toward those goals might be achieved. Setting numerical goals alone causes the first major crack in the system and its connections. The oft-repeated axiom "If it can't be measured, then it can't be managed" is one of the most ludicrous beliefs about measurement. What are we thinking when we say this? (Or are we thinking at all?)

There are hundreds of examples that refute this nonsense, but here's a commonsense example: Let's say we asked parents, "Do you feel that it is important to play with your children?" Most people would agree that playing with children is very important; it encourages their creativity and learning and offers other benefits. What if we asked, "Do you measure the time you play with them?" Most parents would say, "No, why would I do that? I know it is important, and so I spend time with my child whenever possible." We might reply, "Then why not measure it?" After all, the common belief is that if it is truly important, it can and must be measured. But what would we measure: the number of minutes we play? The number of activities? The number of times the child asks a question about the rules of the game?

Metrics aren't always meaningful, and not everything can or should be measured. Deming attributed this insight to Dr. Lloyd Nelson, director of statistical methods at Nashua Corporation: "The most important figures for management of any organization are unknown and unknowable."[9] Measurement mania has thrown many of our systems into decline. Our education system, for example, focuses on measuring, testing, and rewarding teachers with merit pay rather than on building a *system* that encourages joy in learning and develops lifelong learners and responsible contributors to society. How do we measure the joy of a lifelong learner or the contributions one makes to society as a result of that joy of learning? The most important measurements are unknown.

The purpose of measurement is to help us determine whether we are going in the right direction to achieve our organization's strategic goals.

For every decision we make, every project and process we work on, will our work and the metrics we track help us get closer to our goals or further away?

Theory of People, Learning Styles, and Motivation

Results—such as financial results, sales quotas, and customer satisfaction—and variation in results are caused by the environment, by processes, by equipment, by material, and by people. Most of the time, we attribute all results (and variation) to people, particularly the people who are closest to the results.

- We tip a waitress less because the food was improperly prepared (variation in the process) or the service was slow (variation in the environment because two other waitresses called in sick).

- A project manager, whose results are compared to budgets, quota, or goals, is considered successful or unsuccessful based on how well the negotiations went during last year's budgeting meeting.

- Salespeople hold or accelerate sales or sales returns, thus distorting the figures, to meet goals and quotas. For example, if a sales rep meets his or her quota for the period five days early, he or she might hold new sales orders until the next period begins to help ensure that he or she will meet the next period's quota.

Remember, top management is responsible for the system. Employees and project teams work in the system, and while they are responsible for their own behavior, they cannot be held accountable for the results of the system, with its many interdependent parts that often fail to connect.

If an organization and the project teams within it succeed, it is because top management has made a significant commitment to transform the company into a thriving, dynamic, developing, learning organization with a management philosophy grounded in theories, not management fads.

Transformation Is Not Just Change

To *transform* means to change in form, appearance, or structure, or to create something new that has never existed before and perhaps could not have been anticipated. Organizational transformation happens when leaders develop a vision of transformation and a system for continually questioning and challenging beliefs, assumptions, patterns, habits, and paradigms. Leaders who understand this will ask challenging, cutting-edge questions, using the OSC and system diagram, and strive to continually apply management theory through the lens of systems and statistical thinking.

Pak Fresh CEO Joyce Musil-Condon explains it well:

> Becoming a transformational leader is not easy. It's hard to stop doing what you've always done; ask the tough questions; challenge the status quo; admit that you don't know the answers; and focus on delivering value to the customer wants while sustaining the organization.

Organizational transformation occurs first in individuals, then in the organization itself. It requires a change in mindset. It requires leaders to understand systems thinking, statistical thinking and variation, prediction, and the psychology of people and culture. It also demands that leaders take decisive action. Transformation means leading an organization into the unknown. This is why communication, collaboration, rapid learning from projects, and working together toward the aim of the organization are fundamental.

Transformation is the real key to a business's survival and leadership position. An organization that is unable to achieve its potential must transform, which means that first, its leaders must personally transform themselves. To change the organization and to achieve better results, leaders need to think, do, question, and feel differently, not just measure differently. They must challenge their current beliefs, assumptions, and practices.

If leaders succeed in transforming their thinking and actions, their companies may survive, even innovate. If they do not, their organizations' decline and failure is imminent—no matter how hard people work, how brilliant their new ideas are, how efficiently processes flow, or how well project teams collaborate.

Survival, even for Fortune 500 companies, is not guaranteed. In fact, more than half of the companies that appeared in the first Fortune 500 list in the early 1950s no longer make the list.[10] They do not exist as they did 60 years ago. Current success guarantees nothing in the future.

In the 1980s, IBM was floundering. Management guru and author of *Everyday Heroes*, Dr. Perry Gluckman, keenly observed, "IBM is like a big dinosaur; it will just take longer to come to its knees." IBM survived because its new leadership is committed to making transformative, sustainable changes in thinking about and questioning its philosophical approach.[11]

Unfortunately, few individuals understand transformation or why it is an imperative. They don't understand why incremental or transitional change is not enough. Often, people confuse transformation with *any* kind of change, such as change management initiatives, technology breakthroughs, innovation, process improvements, or transitions. The truth is that all transformation is change, but not all change is transformation. Real transformations result in a competitive edge and unparalleled leadership that can make a difference in our society.

Final Thoughts

Leaders can give project managers clear direction by answering three questions:

- What purpose are we trying to accomplish in this organization, and where are we going?
- By what methods will we accomplish our purpose?
- Who are we serving, and how will we know how well we're doing?

It seems as if these few questions should not be too difficult to answer. They are pretty straightforward. But too often, leaders do not do their job. They either do not understand it or they delegate it. A leader's job is to answer these questions clearly and specifically so that all employees understand their roles in the organization. Leadership must be open to learning and listening to their employees and their customers and then adapting and redesigning their organization systematically to deliver better results for today and for the future.

The system diagram and the organizational strategic compass are two leadership tools that are foundational for the communication and clarity needed for all parts of an enterprise to work together to help achieve project and organizational success. Without strategic thinking and regular and effective communication regarding strategy, the organization as a system will struggle to succeed.

Adaptive leadership thinking establishes organizational learning that fosters successful project management and a competitive edge. Implementing a new way of leading takes courage. But an organization cannot succeed without effective leadership guiding project management. Leadership and project management are interdependent. Only together can they deliver profound value to customers!

Notes

1 Nida Backaitis and Marcia Daszko, "Still Ahead of His Time: The Management Philosophy of W. Edwards Deming in the Internet Era," (Santa Clara, CA: Marcia Daszko & Associates, 1995). Available online at http://www.mdaszko.com/articles_01.html (accessed February 6, 2010).
2 Marcia Daszko, "Innovate or Evaporate: How to Create a Sustainable Future," research paper presented at the Deming Research Conference, Fordham University, New York, 2002. Available online at http://mdaszko.com/Article3.pdf (accessed February 20, 2010).
3 Nida Backaitis and Marcia Daszko, "Still Ahead of His Time: The Management Philosophy of W. Edwards Deming in the Internet Era," (Santa Clara, CA: Marcia Daszko & Associates, 1995). Available online at http://www.mdaszko.com/articles_01.html (accessed February 6, 2010).

4   Ibid.

5   W. Edwards Deming, *The New Economics for Industry, Government, Education, Second Edition* (Cambridge, MA: The MIT Press, 2000), 92–115.

6   Ibid., 101.

7   Peter M. Senge, *The Fifth Discipline: The Art & Practice of the Learning Organization* (New York: Doubleday, 2006), 18.

8   Ibid., 19.

9   W. Edwards Deming, *Out of the Crisis* (Cambridge, MA: The MIT Press, 1986).

10 See Fortune 500, "Database of 50 years of Fortune's list of America's largest corporations." Available online at http://money.com/magazines/fortune/fortune500_archive/full/1955/401.html (accessed February 20, 2010).

11 Louis Gerstner, Jr., *Who Says Elephants Can't Dance?* (New York: Harper Collins, 2002).

■ INDEX

Managing Complex Projects: A New Model
Kathleen B. Hass, PMP

For organizations to thrive, indeed to survive, in today's global economy, we must find ways to dramatically improve the performance of large-scale projects. *Managing Complex Projects: A New Model* offers an innovative way of looking at projects and treating them as complex adaptive systems. Applying the principles of complexity thinking will enable project managers and leadership teams to manage large-scale initiatives successfully.

ISBN 978-1-56726-233-9 ■ Product Code B339 ■ 398 pages

How to Save a Failing Project: Chaos to Control
Ralph R. Young, Steven M. Brady, and Dennis C. Nagle, Jr.

Poor project results are all too common and result in dissatisfied customers, users, and project staff. With countless people, goals, objectives, expectations, budgets, schedules, deliverables, and deadlines to consider, it can be difficult to keep projects in focus and on track. *How to Save a Failing Project: Chaos to Control* arms project managers with the tools and techniques needed to address these project challenges. The authors provide guidance to develop a project plan, establish a schedule for execution, identify project tracking mechanisms, and implement turn-around methods to avoid failure and regain control.

ISBN 978-1-56726-239-1 ■ Product Code B391 ■ 234 pages

The Project Manager's Guide to Making Successful Decisions
COL Robert A. Powell, PhD and Dennis M. Buede, PhD

Decision-making is critical in project management. Lack of decision-making knowledge, avoidable mistakes, and improper definitions can negatively impact your company's ability to generate profit. *The Project Manager's Guide to Making Successful Decisions* is a practical handbook that focuses on the significance of project decision-making skills that will allow you to reach workable and effective results. This valuable resource highlights various techniques that facilitate the decision-making process, provides an overview of decision analysis as it relates to project management, and much more!

ISBN 978-1-56726-234-6 ■ Product Code B346 ■ 311 pages

Work Breakdown Structures for Projects, Programs, and Enterprises
Gregory T. Haugan, Ph.D., PMP

The basic concept and use of the work breakdown structure (WBS) are fundamental in project management. In *Work Breakdown Structures for Projects, Programs, and Enterprises*, author Gregory T. Haugan, originator of the widely accepted 100 percent rule, offers an expanded understanding of the WBS concept, illustrating its principles and applications for planning programs as well as its use as an organizing framework at the enterprise level. Through specific examples, this book will help you understand how the WBS aids in the planning and management of all functional areas of project management.

ISBN 978-1-56726-228-5 ■ Product Code B285 ■ 382 pages